HOW TO
PREVENT MISCARRIAGE
AND
OTHER CRISES OF
PREGNANCY

HOW TO
Prevent
Miscarriage
A N D
Other Crises of
Pregnancy

___

STEFAN SEMCHYSHYN, M.D.
AND
CAROL COLMAN

Foreword by Frederick P. Zuspan, M.D.

MACMILLAN • USA

Macmillan General Reference
A Simon & Schuster Macmillan Company
1633 Broadway
New York, NY 10019-6785

This book is not intended as a substitute for the medical advice of a doctor. The reader should regularly consult a doctor in matters relating to her health and that of her unborn child and particularly with respect to any symptoms that may require diagnosis or medical attention.

The names and situations of the patients mentioned in this book have been changed to protect their privacy.

Library of Congress Cataloging-in-Publication Data

Semchyshyn, Stefan.
    How to prevent miscarriage and other crises of pregnancy/Stefan Semchyshyn and Carol Colman; foreword by Frederick P. Zuspan. —
1st Collier Books ed.
        p. cm.
    Reprint. Originally published: New York: Macmillan, c1989.
    ISBN 0-02-036855-0
    1. Miscarriage—Prevention. 2. Pregnancy, Complications of—Prevention. 3. Miscarriage—Popular works. 4. Pregnancy, Complications of—Popular works.   I. Colman, Carol.   II. Title.
[RG648.S44   1990]
618.3'92—dc20   90-1872

Macmillan books are available at special discounts for bulk purchases for sales promotions, premiums, fundraising, or educational use. For details, contact:

Special Sales
Macmillan General Reference
1633 Broadway
New York, NY 10019-6785

10   9   8

Printed in the United States of America

To those who were part of this
experience and to those who are still
seeking to have normal, healthy babies,
the greatest gift of life

Contents

Foreword

How to Prevent Miscarriage and Other Crises of Pregnancy
should be required reading for any woman who is even considering pregnancy; it will arm her with the critical information
she needs to carry her unborn child safely to term and to
protect her own health.

As my former distinguished fellowship student in maternal-
fetal medicine Dr. Stephen Semchyshyn stresses thoughout
this excellent book, good prenatal care begins long before conception. If every woman embarked on a pregnancy in the best
possible health and was aware of the risk factors that could
threaten the health and well-being of her child, there would
be fewer pregnancy losses and more healthy babies born at full
term. If all women were—to borrow an expression used by Dr.
Semchyshyn—"pregnancy literate," that is, aware of the normal progression of a pregnancy and trained to recognize problems early on, they would be able to forge a true partnership
with their physicians and become full-fledged members of the
health care team.

This book also emphasizes the important role of the

perinatologist, or specialist in maternal-fetal medicine. After completing four years of residency training in the field of obstetrics and gynecology following graduation from medical school, the perinatologist spends a minimum of two years in a special fellowship program in maternal-fetal medicine. These highly dedicated, skilled physicians are committed to ensuring that pregnant patients receive the best care possible, and they have access to the most modern, state-of-the-art technology. Dr. Semchyshyn, one of the first physicians who was privileged to receive formal training and be certified in this field, has become a role model of the caring, dedicated practitioner who treats both the physical and emotional wounds associated with miscarriage, stillbirth, and premature labor.

Over the past decade there have been spectacular advances in the field of obstetrics. Although many questions remain unanswered, we now have the skill and the knowledge to help many women who were once described as "hopeless cases" carry safely to term and give birth to healthy, normal babies. This book will help make more women aware of their treatment options and, in turn, will help them become more selective and discerning health care consumers.

I hope that all women contemplating pregnancy will read this book. It will help them to evaluate their situations and to identify and deal with many of the problems that could impair their ability to carry to term. It will help them understand what to expect in the course of their pregnancies, so that they can distinguish between events that are normal and those that are not—and to seek medical intervention, when necessary, at the earliest possible time.

Finally, I think this book will demonstrate that, thanks to recent advances in maternal-fetal medicine, it is now possible for many women—even those who have suffered multiple miscarriages—to carry healthy babies to term.

FREDERICK P. ZUSPAN, M.D.
Professor, Richard L. Meiling Chair
   in Obstetrics and Gynecology,
   The Ohio State University College of Medicine
Editor, *American Journal of Obstetrics
   and Gynecology*
Editor-in-Chief, *OB-GYN Reports*

Acknowledgments

This book has been made possible through the help of too many people to list them all here. First and most important, I would like to thank all the patients who allowed me to share in their experiences and become a part of their successes, providing me with the opportunity to learn and, in turn, to pass my knowledge on to others by writing this book.

I thank God for giving me the vision to know that which is possible and the courage to undertake that which is achievable.

I express my deepest appreciation to those who served as role models and provided me with guidance and caring support: Kaye Hayashidea, Ph.D.; T. Prociw, Ph.D; J. B. Firtsbrook, M.D.; J. V. Sorbara, M.D.; W. J. Hannah, M.D.; T. T. Decyk; M. W. Kronisch, Esq.; and F. P. Zuspan, M.D.

I would also like to thank the following experts for their help: Margaret Eckler, M.S., R.D., consulting nutritionist and certified diabetes educator; Joan Kegerize, M.S., Genetic Counseling, Jersey City Medical Center; Carol Accetta, President, Medical Claims Service Corporation, Union, New Jersey; Louise Rosenberg, certified childbirth educator and labor support person; Neal Rote, Ph.D., Foundation for Blood Research, Portland, Maine; and Marjorie Jaffe, founder, Back in Shape Exercise Studios in New York City.

I am forever grateful to my parents, Ivan and Katarina, who influenced and shaped my philosophy, which helped to make me the physician that I am. I thank my seven brothers and two sisters for their support, love, and sustained encouragement. And I am grateful to my family, Helena, Natalie, and Terry, for their tolerance, love, support, and enduring encouragement.

Finally, I thank Macmillan and its staff, and my literary agent, Richard Curtis, for making this dream a reality.

STEFAN SEMCHYSHYN, M.D.

HOW TO
PREVENT MISCARRIAGE
AND
OTHER CRISES OF
PREGNANCY

Introduction

The Miscarriage Myth

After my first miscarriage, my doctor said, "This is very common. It's just nature's way of aborting a deformed fetus." I took it philosophically and thought to myself, "Oh, well, there's always next time." When I miscarried for the second time, my doctor told me it was just more bad luck—another blighted ovum—and that I should go ahead and try again.

I was devastated by the second loss, but I didn't let myself dwell on it. Everyone was telling me to hurry up and get pregnant again. So I did. After my third miscarriage my doctor finally said, "Gee, maybe something *is* wrong."

I was enraged. Why did I have to lose three babies before anyone would do anything about it?

— Marge, today the mother of a four-year-old daughter

If you've ever suffered a miscarriage, you can undoubtedly identify with Marge's frustration and anger. Therefore, there are two things I want to tell you. One is that you're not alone. One out of four women has experienced the emotional and physical pain of losing a baby. The other thing I want you to know is that there is hope. Marge is now a mother and with proper treatment, I believe most of you will also be able to become mothers.

Not only that, I want those of you who have never miscarried but who, because of your age or medical condition, are at risk of miscarriage, to know that there are ways of preventing a miscarriage from happening in the first place. You need not suffer what Marge and countless other women have suffered. With proper care and treatment, you may be able to carry all of your pregnancies to term.

Contrary to popular belief, miscarriage is not always "nature's way" of ending the life of an embryo or fetus that is not developing properly. In fact, medical studies reveal that in about one-third of all miscarriage cases, the problem is not a defective baby, but a maternal medical problem. In other words, a healthy, normal child could have been born had the mother been able to carry to term.

Moreover, the vast majority of these women—perhaps as many as 90 percent—could have carried to term had their pregnancies been properly managed. Yet, because their problems go undiagnosed and untreated, these women stand a good chance of losing their babies again . . . and again . . . and again.

I am an obstetrician and a high-risk pregnancy specialist. Many of the women I see have already suffered the anguish of numerous pregnancy losses. Some have endured the pain of multiple miscarriages. Some have carried to term only to give birth to a stillborn child. Some have lost babies late in pregnancy as a result of premature labor. Many have spent years going from doctor to doctor looking for answers, but hearing the same antiquated fables about miscarriage that have been passed down through the centuries:

"You're having a run of bad luck."

"If the pregnancy was meant to be, you wouldn't have miscarried."

"Miscarriage is just one of those things, and there's nothing to be done about it."

After three miscarriages, many doctors label these women "habitual aborters" (a term I despise) and give them scant hope of ever having children of their own. Nevertheless, when these same "habitual aborters" follow my treatment program, the overwhelming majority of them (about 95 percent) become mothers. How is this possible?

Although many of my patients claim that I perform miracles, I know that is not the case. All I am doing is performing good medicine, using the most up-to-date techniques available, and teaching my patients how to become active partners in the treatment process and their care.

The real tragedy is that many of these women need not have suffered any miscarriages or premature births. In many cases, simple, obvious problems were overlooked, and telltale symptoms were dismissed as "perfectly normal."

In fairness, I must say that there are doctors who take a first miscarriage as seriously as their patients do. These doctors don't follow the standard medical practice of waiting for their patients to suffer two or three or more miscarriages before taking notice. After the first loss, they work closely with their patients to make sure that the next pregnancy is a successful one. There are even some maverick doctors who, like myself, try to prevent the tragedy of a first miscarriage.

If you're being treated by one of these doctors, you're very lucky, because they are few and far between. Most doctors are inclined to dismiss a woman's first or second miscarriage as a fluke and no cause for alarm. Typically, these doctors will recommend that the patient "give it a few months and then try again." Although this approach may work for the woman who actually was carrying a defective fetus, it is a serious disservice to the woman who miscarried for other, and probably avoidable, reasons. Thus, unless and until a miscarriage can be linked to a fetal abnormality, it should be taken as a warning that something may be hampering a woman's ability to carry to term. What sorts of things might hamper a woman's ability to sustain a pregnancy? I will discuss these in detail in chapter 1, "The Causes of Miscarriage and Premature Birth." At this point, though, I'll note that there are a number of disorders, some obvious and some hidden, that could be at work. For example, a woman may be suffering from a hormonal imbalance or an infection that makes it impossible for her to sustain a pregnancy without treatment. Or, a uterine abnormality or a weak cervix might be responsible. In cases such as these, maintaining a pregnancy requires close monitoring by both the physician and the patient, and, of course, treatment. Without special attention, the prognosis for a successful pregnancy is poor. With proper care, the outlook is much brighter.

Unfortunately, old attitudes die hard. There are some doctors who may still believe that as soon as a pregnancy runs into serious problems, all they can do is tell their patients to get some rest and let nature take its course. They believe that if a woman is going to miscarry, there's nothing that can or should be done to prevent it. Therefore, they feel that the patient is better off if the pregnancy is terminated—either through spontaneous or induced abortion—as soon as possible.

This probably was the right advice—yesterday. During the past decade, however, there have been spectacular advances in modern maternal-fetal medicine. Today there are relatively safe medications and innovative medical procedures that make it possible for women with even the most severe problems to have healthy babies. Yet, many doctors cling to outmoded notions of what is and isn't possible and of what is "good for the mother." These notions fail to reflect the current reality.

Some doctors may believe that it is easier for the patient (and perhaps in some cases easier for themselves) to allow a troubled pregnancy to end. Their belief is that the next pregnancy will be less complicated and have a happier ending. Unfortunately, they are not always right: In many cases the problem that caused the first miscarriage will cause another.

In light of the fact that at least 15 percent of all couples have difficulty conceiving, there may not even be a next time. In addition, more and more women are postponing childbearing into their thirties and beyond, a time when fertility starts to diminish. These women, in particular, may not get another chance at pregnancy and therefore, *every pregnancy must be made to count.*

Many obstetricians and patients may be reluctant to save a troubled pregnancy for fear that they are interfering with nature's attempt to abort a defective fetus. But, thanks to recent advances in the field of genetic testing and ultrasound (a noninvasive procedure that allows physicians to look inside the womb at virtually no risk to either mother or baby), much of the guesswork can be eliminated by the sixteenth week of pregnancy. If a troubled pregnancy can be sustained until these tests are performed, the mother and doctor can then make an informed decision on whether to continue the pregnancy.

Some doctors may argue that the cost of running a battery of diagnostic tests on every miscarriage patient would be so prohibitive, and the results so confusing, that the best approach is still to do nothing. These doctors are only half right. There are literally hundreds of diagnostic tests that can be used to determine the cause of miscarriage and obviously, we can't subject every patient to every test. However, by working closely with the patient—by carefully evaluating her medical history and reviewing any symptoms that led up to the miscarriage—we can often come up with a diagnosis or narrow down the possibilities to the point where we can order a single test or only a few of them to confirm a suspected diagnosis.

Of course, there are times when, despite our best efforts, the cause of a miscarriage is never identified. Although in these cases we doctors can't offer the patient any concrete medical explanation for her loss, we can make it a point to work closely with her to ensure that subsequent pregnancies are more successful. Simply telling her to "try again" is not enough. We must learn and benefit from past experiences as much as possible.

My purpose in telling you all this—and in writing this book—is not to make you frightened or angry, or to alienate you from your doctor. Rather, my purpose is to provide you with a program for working together with your doctor as a team to achieve a successful pregnancy and give birth to a normal, healthy child.

My purpose is to encourage you patients, who are, after all, consumers of medical services, to make more demands on the medical profession, so that doctors are forced to shed archaic notions that hamper their ability to perform well and fully serve their patients.

My purpose is to wipe out what I regard as the main culprit in miscarriage and premature birth: pregnancy illiteracy. As the full-time caretaker of her pregnancy, a woman must learn to read her body and to distinguish between the normal aches and "growing pains" of pregnancy and the more menacing signs of miscarriage and premature labor.

Finally, my purpose is to spare all women the psychological and physical toll of miscarriage and premature labor, and to eliminate the tragic and wasteful loss of healthy, desperately wanted children.

I am going to spend the balance of this book discussing the causes of miscarriage, how to determine whether you are at risk of suffering a miscarriage, and how you and your doctor can work to avert a miscarriage. But first I want to introduce you to some medical terms and concepts that I will be using throughout the book.

When I use the term *high-risk pregnancy,* I am referring to women who, because of their age, lifestyle, or previous medical problems, are at greater risk of suffering a miscarriage or delivering prematurely. About 15 percent of all expectant mothers are considered high risk.

When I talk about *carrying a pregnancy to term,* I am referring to a forty-week gestational period beginning at the first day of the last menstrual period. Since the actual date of conception can rarely truly be verified, doctors prefer to date a pregnancy from the last menstrual period.

Although most people use the word *miscarriage* as a general term to describe the loss of an unborn child, they are not entirely correct. In more precise terms, a miscarriage refers to a loss that occurs up until the twentieth week of pregnancy. If the baby is born after the twentieth week and does not survive, it is called a *stillbirth.*

A *premature birth* occurs if a live infant is born prior to the thirty-seventh week of pregnancy.

In medical jargon, the term "miscarriage" is not used because it is considered to be too vague. Rather, pregnancy losses are called *spontaneous abortions.* There are five different categories of spontaneous abortions as defined below.

- *Threatened abortion:* A threatened abortion is suspected when any vaginal bleeding or bloody discharge occurs during the first half of pregnancy. About 25 percent of all pregnant women experience bleeding during the first trimester.
- *Inevitable abortion:* Inside the mother's womb, or uterus, the fetus is encased in protective membranes and surrounded by fluid. During the first half of pregnancy, if the membranes are severely ruptured and the cervix, the neck of the womb, begins to dilate or thin out, it is nearly impossible to save the pregnancy.
- *Incomplete abortion:* Incomplete abortion occurs when part of the product of conception—the conceptus—is retained in the uterus, although it is usually expelled on its own. If it is not, a D and C (dilatation and curettage), a gentle scraping of the uterine wall, may be required. If the uterus is not cleaned out, the mother runs the risk of developing an infection or hemorrhaging.
- *Missed abortion:* Fetal death usually results in a spontaneous abortion. However, if the fetus is not miscarried within eight weeks of its death, it is a called a missed abortion. If all the pregnancy material is not expelled on its own, a D and C may be required to prevent an infection; also, the patient must have her uterus emptied before she can resume menstruation.
- *Habitual abortion:* Habitual abortion refers to repeat, spontaneous abortions. (As I said earlier, I find this term offensive because I feel it stigmatizes the unfortunate woman who, through no fault of her own, has had to endure the agony of multiple losses.)

Although my practice is confined to high-risk women, I believe that the style of care that I am advocating can benefit all women, high risk or not. Many—but not all—high risk pregnancy specialists such as myself already provide the kind of patient care that I describe in this book. However, I feel that such basics as patient education and involvement in the pregnancy and birthing process should be offered by *all* obstetricians to *all* expectant mothers so that low-risk pregnancy can be kept low risk and high-risk pregnancy can be transformed into a normal experience.

The Tragedy of Premature Birth

There's so much ignorance about premature labor. A classic example is a recent *Newsweek* cover story on premies with the headline, "The miracles begin at one pound." Well, I have one of these so-called "miracle babies." She was born at 22 weeks. She's blind and she's retarded and she's going to need special care for the rest of her life. Before we brought her home, her hospital bill was over $250,000 and her continued care requires about $30,000 a year. For my second pregnancy, I wanted to be sure that it didn't happen again. I found a doctor who believed in prevention. Despite a very difficult pregnancy, I carried my son to term and he's perfectly healthy. The hospital bill was nominal. To me he's the real "miracle" baby. But no one is doing magazine articles about prematurity prevention.

— Cathy, mother of a four-year-old daughter, born at twenty-two weeks, and a two-year-old son, born at term

Although a large part of my practice is dedicated to the prevention of miscarriage, I also devote a considerable amount of time to helping my patients avoid premature birth. In fact, to me, the problems of miscarriage and premature birth are so interrelated that I regard them as essentially one and the same. As we saw earlier, the difference, really, is one of timing. A pregnancy that terminates prior to the twentieth week of pregnancy is regarded as a miscarriage. One that terminates between the twentieth and thirty-seventh weeks is regarded as either a premature delivery, if the baby survives, or a stillbirth.

In the United States, about 10 percent of all babies are born prematurely. These babies are at great risk of serious medical complications, possibly culminating in death. Prematurity is the number one killer of infants. It is responsible for 80 percent of all newborn deaths (in the United States alone, some 32,000 every year). It is also responsible for serious disabilities, including such lifelong handicaps as brain damage and blindness.

Prematurity is so dangerous because the baby is born before he can live independently outside the protective environment of the womb. A healthy, full-term baby is able to function independently. He is able to breathe, digest food, eliminate waste, and perform the basic human functions necessary for survival.

Not so with a premature infant. The baby who is born before nature intended him to live on his own is faced with many potentially lethal problems. He may not be able to perform the simplest of tasks, such as eating or breathing. His lungs may not be mature enough to inhale and exhale. His intestinal tract may not be developed enough to absorb food. Critical organs, such as his liver, may not be fully functional.

Extraordinary medical measures are often required to sustain the premature infant. For example, the baby may be taken to a neonatal intensive care unit, placed on a respirator to breathe, and fed intravenously until his body is capable of assuming those functions. Although these lifesaving measures are necessary, they are not without risk. A newborn's lungs are fragile and can easily be ruptured by the respirator. If too much oxygen is administered, he could be blinded for life. The needle used to introduce an IV can also introduce infection.

The cost of this care can be astronomical. Depending on the degree of prematurity and the duration of hospitalization, one "premie" can run up a bill of hundreds of thousands of dollars before he goes home. If he is permanently disabled, the cost of his subsequent medical care can reach the million-dollar mark. While some insurance companies may pick up most or all of the tab for the intensive care nursery and the necessary aftercare, many do not. The financial burden falls squarely on the parents. Despite all we hear about the wonders of the intensive care nursery, in most cases, until a baby is full term, the best nursery is still the mother's womb and every effort should be made to keep him there. So much for "miracle babies."

Fortunately, with proper medical treatment, most premature births can be prevented. I work with many patients who are considered to be at high risk of delivering prematurely. Those who have delivered prematurely before are at higher risk of doing so again. Others have medical problems that may make them more prone to early delivery. Yet, less than 3 percent of my patients deliver prior to the thirty-seventh week.

I approach the problem of premature delivery the same way that I approach miscarriage. I rely both on up-to-date medical science and on heightened patient awareness and participation. Every one of my patients knows how to monitor her own body for any abnormalities that could signal the onset of premature labor. I can count on my patients to bring a problem to my attention while there is still time to do something about it. Time is of the essence because if a patient detects the onset of labor early in the game, there is much we can do to stop it and sustain the pregnancy until the baby has a better chance of survival outside the womb. However, if labor progresses too far, there is nothing we can do to prevent the birth of the baby.

Unfortunately, most women wait too long before seeking treatment. Only one in ten women who are hospitalized for premature labor gets there in time to be helped. It should be pointed out, though, that it's not always the patients who are slow to seek treatment. Very often, physicians fail to pick up the signs of premature labor, and are quick to dismiss complaints about aches and pains as perfectly normal. By the time the physician recognizes the problem, the baby is ready to be delivered and nothing can be done to prevent it. Later, in chapter 5, I will explain how to distinguish between what's normal and what's not, and how to bring symptoms to the attention of your doctor.

What My Miscarriage Prevention Program Is All About

The difference between my past pregnancies and all the others was that this time, I felt in control. During my other pregnancies, whenever I had a problem, I used to debate about whether or not I should call the doctor. This time, I knew how to take care of myself, I knew what to watch out for, and at the first hint of a problem, I called Dr. Semchyshyn and we took care of it together. I learned so much about my body that my husband used to tease me and say that I was starting to sound like a doctor.

— Mary Ann, two miscarriages, now mother of a
   three-year-old girl

My prescription for a successful pregnancy is really very simple, so simple in fact, that it can be described in one word: prevention. Here's what I mean.

If we identify and treat little problems early on, chances are they will not develop into big problems that are much more difficult to control.

If patients are encouraged to practice good prenatal medicine in and out of the doctor's office, chances are they will avoid most of the complications that can threaten the health and well-being of their babies.

Although my approach is hardly radical, it is unusual. The practice of medicine in general, and obstetrics in particular, is based on crisis intervention, not crisis prevention. My goal is to intervene before problems reach crisis proportion.

In order to achieve this goal, patients must be educated so they can work effectively with their physicians.

It's not enough for a doctor to hand a pregnant patient a prescription for prenatal vitamins or a pamphlet on pregnancy and tell her to call him if she has any problems. Someone who is not pregnancy literate is not going to be able to distinguish between the normal bodily changes that occur during pregnancy and the more ominous ones that portend trouble. Every woman needs to be thoroughly educated so she can immediately detect when something isn't right.

When an expectant mother and her doctor work together this way, I call them "partners in pregnancy," a relationship that is fully explored in chapter 4. And I mean it when I say "partners." As you will see, my aim is not to push doctors out of the picture. On the contrary, a woman who is pregnancy literate will be in a much better position to keep her doctor informed and involved.

Patient education also means alerting women who are at risk of miscarriage and premature birth to the possibility that their pregnancies may run into trouble long before they suffer a pregnancy loss or give birth prematurely. In many cases, high-risk women may be able to dramatically improve their prospects for success by taking certain precautionary measures. Chapter 1, "The Causes of Miscarriage and Premature Birth," will arm you with everything you need to know about risk factors before you get started. Despite our best efforts to avoid problems, sometimes they arise. Fortunately, today's obstetrician has an arsenal of treatment options that can help sustain even the most troubled pregnancy. In chapter 8 I explain, in terms that you will understand, some of the most recent medical breakthroughs that are making the possibility of motherhood a reality for women who only knew the pain of miscarriage.

I have included a section, "Starting Over: A Game Plan for Success," in chapter 3, especially for women who have suffered a pregnancy loss. I think that a woman who reads this chapter will no longer accept the explanation that her miscarriage was "just one of those things." She will demand that other factors be considered and she will insist on special attention during her next pregnancy.

While my program stresses the patient/doctor relationship, it also recognizes that there are other people who have much to contribute. In my own practice, with the help of my patients, I have established a patient network in which women who have already experienced a successful pregnancy, or who are in a more advanced stage of pregnancy, offer help and emotional support to other pregnant women. I describe this patient network as well as other sources of support in chapter 10, "With a Little Help from Your Friends."

I am proud of the success rate of my program and the fact that 97.5 percent of the time, my patients are able to fulfill their dreams of becoming mothers.

As good as that percentage may be, I feel it is still not good enough. I grieve for the 2.5 percent of my patients whom I am unable to help. But I have not given up hope for them, and I hope that they haven't either. Every day, new information is being discovered about the causes of miscarriage, and new treatments are being devised to help sustain troubled pregnancies.

It's important to remember that just a decade ago, many of the women whom I have been able to help would have been rightfully regarded as hopeless cases. Given the advances we have witnessed in the past decade, I believe that there will come a day when virtually every woman who wants to become a mother will be able to achieve that goal.

ONE

The Causes of Miscarriage and Premature Birth

You get sick and tired of hearing how "normal" it is to miscarry. "Normal" is getting pregnant and having a baby nine months later. I wanted some straight answers!

— Wendy, two miscarriages, mother of twin three-year-old boys

There is nothing as frustrating as losing baby after baby and not even knowing why it's happening. Although we don't always have the answers, we do know a great deal more today about the causes of miscarriage than we did a mere decade ago.

We now know that much of what was once dismissed as "nature's way" could be any number of problems that, if identified early enough, can be successfully treated. We also know that some women, because of their age, certain medical problems, or other factors, are at "high risk" of suffering a miscarriage.

In this chapter I will explain some of the causes of miscarriage and I will describe these high-risk factors. This will help those of you who have suffered a miscarriage to understand what went wrong. It will help those of you who are at high risk to identify that fact and understand why. Then I can turn to the question that I know you want answered: What can I and my doctor do to avoid a loss?

Chromosomal Abnormality

Chromosomal aberrations, an abnormal rearrangement of chromosomes, are responsible for:

- 60 percent of all spontaneous abortions in the first half of the first trimester
- 15 to 20 percent of all miscarriages in the second half of the first trimester
- 10 percent of all miscarriages in the second trimester.

Because genetics plays such a critical role in early miscarriage, I have devoted the next chapter to this important subject.

Over Thirty-five: Prime Time or Over the Hill?

When I was thirty-eight I had two miscarriages in a row and I was very worried. I felt that time was running out and there wouldn't be too many chances left to have a baby. I couldn't help feeling guilty that maybe I had waited too long, maybe I shouldn't have put off motherhood so I could pursue my career. Fortunately, I found a doctor who realized that I had a hormonal problem that had caused the miscarriages and once it was treated, I was able to carry to term. Now that I'm a

mother, I'm glad I waited. I believe that I'm a better
mother now than I would have been ten years ago because
I'm more mature, and better able to cope with the
emotional demands of raising children.

— Joyce, mother of a three-year-old boy

Recently, Sharon, a thirty-four-year-old M.B.A., came to me for
a consultation. Like so many other women of her generation,
Sharon had deferred marriage and motherhood to pursue a
career. Secure in her job as marketing director for a local
bank—and very much in love with a colleague at work—
Sharon was finally ready to take on the responsibility of marriage and family. The wedding was set for the following
month.

What should have been one of the happiest times of
Sharon's life was fast turning into a nightmare. While she and
her husband-to-be, Richard, wanted to spend one carefree
year together before starting a pregnancy, both sets of potential grandparents and even some well-meaning friends were
urging the couple not to wait even a second longer than they
had to.

"If you don't have children by the time you're thirty-five,
you might as well forget it," Sharon's mother warned her.
"After that, it's just too dangerous."

Concerned by her mother's remarks, Sharon did some research on midlife pregnancy. Much to her dismay, she learned
that pregnancies involving women over thirty-five are classified as "high risk," a term she found ominous and un-
settling.

Sharon's dilemma is hardly unusual. Over the past decade,
I have seen a growing number of women in their mid- to late
thirties and even early forties contemplating motherhood for
the first time. In fact, according to the U.S. Census Bureau, first
birth rates for women in their early thirties more than doubled
between 1972 and 1982. What's even more interesting is the
fact that rates for women in their late thirties soared 83 percent during the same period.

My first remarks to Sharon put a smile on her face. I told
her that I had worked with many women her age and older

who had undergone successful pregnancies. Before she decided whether or not to postpone her pregnancy another year, I wanted to give her the facts so she could make an educated decision.

Despite my generally positive experiences with older mothers, I told Sharon that these pregnancies were at greater risk for certain problems than those of younger mothers. First of all, by the time a woman reaches thirty, her ability to become pregnant gradually begins to decrease. There are several reasons for this decline in fertility, including the relationship between age and the number of eggs a woman has left for ovulation.

When a woman is born, she has about a million tiny eggs in her ovaries. By the time she reaches adolescence, the number has dropped to about half a million. When she begins to menstruate, about fifty of these eggs begin to ripen each month in preparation for ovulation, although most degenerate prior to ovulation, when typically only one ripened ovum is released. For a pregnancy to occur, the ovum must be fertilized by a sperm. As a woman ages, the number of ova or eggs in her body decreases. As her fertility declines, there may be months when, although she gets a menstrual period, she may not be ovulating or releasing the ripened ovum, thus making pregnancy impossible.

Even if a woman over thirty-five has no problems with ovulation, there may be other factors interfering with pregnancy. For example, tubal occlusion, a blockage of the fallopian tubes caused by the buildup of scar tissue from previous infections or surgery, could be preventing the ripened egg from uniting with the sperm. Although this condition can happen to women of any age, the "older" woman is at greater risk simply because she has had more years of exposure to potential problems like infections and more time to develop other problems that might require surgery.

One of those problems is endometriosis, a disorder that often presents itself in midlife and can affect fertility. For some unknown reason, little blood cysts are formed in and around the uterus, tubes, and ovaries. The cells in these cysts are like those that normally line the uterus and can cause extensive scarring. Endometriosis, which can be quite painful, can in many cases be successfully treated with hormonal therapy.

Despite these potential roadblocks to fertility, I told Sharon that the majority of women thirty-five and older should have no trouble becoming pregnant. The story, however, doesn't end there. Once pregnant, these mothers-to-be have a whole new set of concerns.

The Health of the Baby The likelihood of birth defects increases with age. For example, Down's syndrome, a disease resulting in mental retardation and other severe medical problems, strikes only 1 in 1,600 children born to women in their early twenties. By the time a woman reaches thirty-five, however, she has a 1-in-365 chance of birthing a Down's baby. At age forty, that risk jumps to 1 in 100 and at age forty-five, 1 in 32. Down's syndrome, caused by a chromosomal abnormality, is one of the 350 genetic disorders that can be screened by amniocentesis. To be on the safe side, I advise expectant mothers over thirty-five or those with a history of genetic problems in their family to consult with a genetic counselor.

The Health of the Mother Although pregnancy is a natural and normal phenomenon, it does put an enormous strain on a woman's body. To nourish and care for the new life, every organ in every system is subjected to about 50 percent more work than normal. For most women, it's a labor of love; nevertheless, it can be very taxing.

Unfortunately, as we age, some of our organ systems weaken or stop functioning as well as they did when we were younger. Therefore, the physical stress on an older expectant mother may be greater than on a younger one.

Although age may bring wisdom, patience, and other attributes of a good mother, it is often accompanied by physical problems such as obesity, diabetes, and high blood pressure, conditions that, as we will see, increase the risks to pregnancy. Consequently, the thirty-five-plus mother is slightly more prone to miscarriage, premature birth, dystocia—prolonged and painful labor that does not progress normally—and cesarean delivery. In fact, one in four women over thirty-five undergoes cesarean delivery as opposed to one in five for all women. Although many of these cesareans may be necessary, I believe that many are not. In the case of the older mother, at the first sign of trouble, many well-meaning doctors may go in and take the baby on the theory that they can't afford to take any risk with what may be a woman's last chance at motherhood. In fact, doctors often use the phrase "premium baby" when describing these children. I find this attitude to be extremely distasteful for two reasons. First, I believe that surgical delivery puts the mother at greater risk, not only from the surgery itself but from all the complications, such as infection, that can develop afterwards. Second, whether the mother is seventeen or thirty-seven, all babies are "premium," and the survival of one should not be more important than the survival of another.

Despite all the complications that can occur in a "prime-time" pregnancy, I feel the real issue is not the mother's age but the mother's state of health. If she is generally healthy, of normal weight, doesn't smoke or abuse alcohol or drugs, and doesn't have any medical problems such as diabetes or high blood pressure, the prognosis for her pregnancy is excellent. In fact, I feel that an older but more motivated mother-to-be who takes her pregnancy seriously and is committed to a positive outcome will often fare better than someone twenty years her junior who may not be emotionally prepared for the experience.

I told Sharon that when it comes to pregnancy, mental health is often as important as physical health. If becoming pregnant too soon would place her under a great deal of stress, then perhaps waiting six months to a year might make more sense. That's just what Sharon did. Two years later, the couple had a son after an uneventful pregnancy.

Obesity

Obesity is defined as being 20 percent above your ideal body weight. It sounds like a lot, and yet about 35 million Americans are considered obese. If you're seriously overweight, I feel it is desirable to postpone pregnancy until your weight is within normal range. How do you know whether or not your weight is normal? Here's a method of determining ideal body weight often used by professional dieticians. On average, a five-foot-tall woman should weigh about 100 pounds, give or take 10 pounds either way. For every additional inch over five feet, a woman should allow herself an additional 5 pounds. A 10 percent variation of the total body weight, either up or down the scale, still puts you safely within the normal range. For example, using this formula, a 5-foot, 4-inch woman should weigh about 120 pounds, plus or minus 12 pounds. If she weighs more than 24 pounds over her ideal weight, she would be considered obese.

Obesity can wreak havoc on a pregnancy. First, it puts the mother at greater risk of high blood pressure and diabetes, two disorders that can seriously affect her health as well as the health of her unborn child. Second, obesity masks a lot of problems. Since overweight people tend to have elevated blood pressure, it makes it difficult for a doctor to discern whether a patient is normally hypertensive, or whether she's developing a complication of pregnancy. By the time he figures out the difference, the fetus could be in extreme distress.

Obesity also makes it nearly impossible to perform the necessary physical examinations to detect such critical information as the presence of a fetal heartbeat or the size or position of the baby. Consequently, these mothers-to-be may be forced to undergo more ultrasound—a noninvasive procedure that enables the physician to look inside the womb—and additional prenatal tests than other prospective mothers. Although I believe most of these tests are harmless, I don't believe that they should ever be given unnecessarily.

Finally, excess weight can camouflage a serious symptom such as swelling that could indicate preeclampsia, a potentially fatal condition that I describe in greater detail later in this chapter.

One word of warning. If you're already pregnant, don't diet. In fact, you'll still need to put on some weight to ensure your baby's well-being, but not as much as the average mother-to-be. Your doctor will probably recommend that you restrict your weight gain to about 15 pounds. If he doesn't bring up the subject, however, make sure you do. Our dietary recommendations in the section "Good Nutrition: Building a Firm Foundation" in chapter 6 will also be helpful.

Hormonal Insuffiency

Although there are many hormones in the body, when it comes to pregnancy "hormonal insufficiency" usually refers to an inadequate supply of progesterone. Progesterone plays a critical role in pregnancy and if the body is not producing enough—and if the woman is not supplementing her supply through outside sources—the pregnancy could run into serious trouble. Produced first by the corpus luteum and later by the placenta, progesterone helps to relax the uterus to prevent cramping and contractions. An inadequate level of progesterone can lead to early miscarriage. Spotting, bleeding, or menstrual-type cramps are some of the signs that the level of progesterone may be too deficient to sustain the pregnancy.

History of Infertility

After seven years of infertility, two miscarriages, exploratory surgery and major corrective surgery, my blood test came back positive. I was pregnant. After all those years, you'd think I would have been thrilled, but instead I was terrified. I didn't want to lose another baby.

— Ellen, mother of a five-year-old girl

Going from an infertility problem to a "high-risk" pregnancy seems to be a bitter reward for enduring all those years of anguish and disappointment. The last thing you want to hear is that your hard-won pregnancy is even the slightest bit precarious. While it's important for you to feel relaxed and confident about your ability to carry to term, it is equally important for you and your doctor to be prepared to tackle any possible problems that may crop up.

But the fact is that if you were one of the 15 percent of all couples who were classified as "infertile," you are at greater risk of miscarriage and premature birth. Women with a history of infertility are more likely to have undergone diagnostic workups involving invasive procedures that could have created additional problems. A dilatation and curettage (D and C) performed for diagnostic or therapeutic reasons could also, in the process, have weakened the cervix. A laparoscopy done to determine the degree of tubal occlusion or blockage also could have caused additional scarring.

Furthermore, the condition that was causing the infertility itself could also interfere with the mother's ability to sustain the pregnancy. For instance, as we will see in greater detail later in this chapter, vaginal infections that may interfere with conception may also flare up again during pregnancy and cause a miscarriage. Similarly, as we have just seen, some women have difficulty conceiving because of a hormonal deficiency. If such a woman does become pregnant notwithstanding the deficiency, the pregnancy is likely to be short-lived unless the deficiency is corrected.

There's another compelling reason for couples who have been treated for infertility to be especially careful after they conceive. They may not have had a fertility problem at all. Their problem may be that of early, recurring miscarriages. Recent studies show that nearly 75 percent of all conceptions are chemical pregnancies—that is, although the egg and sperm have united, the pregnancy ends before the fertilized egg is securely embedded in the uterine wall and the menstrual cycle is suspended. In many cases, the mother doesn't know that she is pregnant.

Why does this happen? In many cases, this probably occurs because of a defect in the union of the sperm and the egg—the so-called blighted ovum—preventing proper growth.

There are many other reasons why these pregnancies may be short-lived. During the second half of the menstrual cycle, the corpus luteum that forms in the ovary after fertilization begins to produce progesterone. Inadequate production of progesterone by the corpus luteum may prevent the uterus from developing a lining sufficient to accommodate the pregnancy. As a result, the fertilized egg lacks the necessary fertile ground for it to take root. In some cases, the fertilized egg may never reach the uterus and a faulty fallopian tube may be the culprit. The tiny cilia that propel the fertilized egg through the tube may not be functioning properly. Or a tubal occlusion caused by a previous infection or surgery may be blocking its progress.

The only symptom of a chemical pregnancy may be a history of unexplained infertility, or an unusually heavy, late period.

Recently, some highly sensitive tests have been developed to detect pregnancy-related hormonal changes shortly after conception. These tests make it possible to diagnose pregnancy earlier than ever before. I feel that couples with a history of fertility problems should take advantage of these testing methods so that they will know whether their problem is difficulty in conceiving or difficulty in carrying. A mother-to-be who has a tendency to miscarry shortly after conception may require early intervention to tide her over a critical period.

Thus, couples with fertility problems of any type need to be especially vigilant about protecting their pregnancies. That's why I believe that infertility patients should be treated by a high-risk pregnancy specialist after they conceive. Given the complex nature of medicine today, no one can be an expert in everything. I feel very strongly that these patients, who have already experienced so much heartache, deserve the best medical care possible. (I practice what I preach. I don't treat infertility; rather I refer patients with the problem to qualified people who do.) With the proper medical management, most of these couples will be able to fulfill their dream of becoming parents.

History of Previous Miscarriage

Lightning *can* strike twice in the same place. Women who have miscarried once stand a greater chance of miscarrying again.

The reason why is fairly obvious. Unless it has been corrected, the same problem that has plagued a previous pregnancy can crop up again in all subsequent pregnancies. For example, until it is successfully treated, a simple problem like a hormonal imbalance or a backward-tilted uterus can cause miscarriage after miscarriage. If the mother requires a D and C, or if the miscarriage occurs after fourteen weeks, it can weaken the cervix, increasing the odds that the mother will miscarry again.

As I often say in this book, when it comes to miscarriage, prevention is the best medicine. That's why I feel it's imperative to get good medical care before embarking on another pregnancy.

If you have experienced a miscarriage, be sure to read the section in chapter 3 titled "Starting Over: A Game Plan for Success." It will provide you with critical information that could help prevent another loss.

History of Premature Birth

If you've already delivered one baby prematurely (between 20 and 37 weeks of gestation), you have a 30 percent chance of doing it again. Depending on the cause of the prematurity, your next baby might be delivered even earlier than the previous one.

Whatever triggered the premature labor the first time might strike again. (Hopefully, this time, you and your doctor will be ready for it.) There is also a possibility that a new problem might have developed as a result of the previous premature labor, such as a weakened or incompetent cervix.

Parents who have already undergone the frightening experience of a premature birth may be wary of trying again. Whenever I encounter patients with these fears, I always remind them that despite the risk, the odds are still in their favor. Even if they don't take any preventive steps, they still have a 70 percent chance of carrying to term. I believe, however, that by following a sound prematurity prevention program with your physician, as I do with my patients, you can greatly improve those odds.

Maternal Illness

I was born with a congenital heart condition and I was told that it could get worse if I got pregnant. But there was never any doubt in my mind that I would try to have children. All my life, all I ever wanted was a family. You have to weigh the risks and decide what you want out of life. For me, it was unacceptable not to have children.

— Cheryl, mother of a four-year-old girl and a two-year-old boy

History of Serious Illness

Four years ago, a kidney transplant patient who had gotten pregnant despite her doctor's objections asked me if I would manage her pregnancy. "My doctor thinks I'm crazy to do this, but more than anything else, I want a baby," she explained.

After reviewing her case, she was greatly relieved when I said, "You can tell your doctor that I must be as crazy as you are, because I think we're going to make it!"

And we did. Eight months later, after a moderately difficult pregnancy, she gave birth to a beautiful and healthy baby girl. Since then she has had another full-term baby.

My purpose is not to encourage women with serious medical problems who have been advised not to get pregnant to ignore their doctors' warnings. That would be both foolish and dangerous. However, I want these women to know that thanks to recent medical advances, with proper care and close physician supervision, some of them have a good chance of having babies. In my practice, I have treated women with histories of heart disease, kidney failure, and even cancer. These pregnancies are not without risk to mother and baby, and therefore they must be carefully monitored by a physician who is familiar with both obstetrics and the mother-to-be's particular medical problem. Your best bet is to ask your specialist for a referral. In some cases, you will need to be treated by an obstetrician and a specialist familiar with your case.

One word of warning: If you're taking any medication, before conceiving your child be sure to check with your doctor whether it is safe to use during pregnancy.

Illness During Pregnancy

Outside of pregnancy, infections that are often accompanied by high fever, such as flu, are more of an inconvenience than a serious threat to your health. In fact, unless you're very sick, you may not even feel it is necessary to call your doctor. However, during pregnancy, it's an entirely different matter. Any infection that causes a fever of over 101 degrees—especially during the first trimester—can jeopardize your pregnancy and seriously compromise the health of your baby. Therefore, at the first sign of fever, call your doctor for instructions.

TORCH COMPLEX

TORCH complex is an obstetrical term that refers to several infections that can harm your baby, inside or outside of the womb. Review this list carefully. If you suspect that you have a problem, it's best to consult your physician before embarking on a pregnancy. If you're already pregnant, it's even more critical that you alert him to a possible complication before it becomes a full-blown crisis.

T—Toxoplasmosis   It's an old wives' tale that a jealous cat will not hesitate to jump into a newborn's crib and "suck the air" out of the baby. In reality, the time to worry about the family feline is before the baby is even born. The real culprit is not the cat, but a parasite it may carry that causes a disease called toxoplasmosis. Toxoplasmosis produces high fever and flu-like symptoms in humans. If contracted by a pregnant woman, the disease can result in brain damage and blindness for her baby. Cats contract this parasite from infected rodents and, in turn, spread the organism through their stool. Household cats that never leave the confines of their homes pose little risk, since they are probably not exposed to carriers. To be on the safe side, however, let other family members change the kitty litter during your pregnancy. Needless to say, stay away from any stray or unknown cats.

Before pregnancy, a simple blood test can determine if you've already been exposed to toxoplasmosis and are therefore immune to this disease. If you find out that you are immune, it's one less thing to worry about. If you learn that you're not, don't be thrown into a panic. Do be extra cautious, however, when handling your cat.

When it comes to toxoplasmosis, cats are not the only culprits. The parasite can also be picked up from infected pork or lamb. This doesn't mean that you should avoid eating these meats, only that you should make sure they're well cooked.

O—Others   Other infections, ranging from mumps to influenza to chlamydia, a sexually transmitted disease, can create a hostile womb environment. The following is a list of some of the more common infections that can threaten the health and well-being of both mother and baby.

Pelvic Inflammatory Disease (PID):   PID refers to a group of sexually transmitted diseases, caused by bacteria or viruses, that begin as vaginal infections and, if untreated, can spread to tubes and ovaries, causing infertility and in some cases, miscarriage, premature birth, and infant death. Since many of these diseases are difficult to detect, when it comes to PID prevention is the best medicine. If you have been in a long-term, monogamous relationship, you probably have little to fear. If not, outside of pregnancy, barrier method contraception (condoms) should be used as a defense against these invading microorganisms. If you are already pregnant, be especially vigilant about monitoring your body for even the slightest clues that may indicate the presence of PID. Some of the more common PIDs include the following:

1. *Chlamydia:*   With an estimated 4 million new cases annually (reporting is not mandatory), chlamydia has the dubious honor of being the nation's number one sexually transmit-

ted disease (STD). Caused by a bacterium, chlamydia has been implicated in miscarriage, premature birth, and sudden infant death syndrome (SIDS). Fortunately, it can be successfully treated with antibiotics. Unfortunately, as with other STDs, there are few recognizable symptoms, and many women may have contracted the disease without even knowing it. A slightly irritating yellowish discharge, abdominal pain, and slight bleeding upon intercourse are usually the only signs that the infection is present. However, some women may experience no symptoms at all. If you have a history of chlamydia, tell your doctor so he can test you for the infection either prior to pregnancy or early in pregnancy.

2. *Gonorrhea:* Unlike chlamydia, all cases of gonorrhea must be reported to local public health departments and theoretically all sexual partners of the victims of this STD should be notified. However, public health officials admit that the 1 million reported cases of gonorrhea do not reflect the actual number of Americans who have contracted this disease. Sadly, many of the women who may have this disease don't even know it. The only symptom a woman may experience is a slight difficulty urinating and a slightly irritating vaginal discharge. These benign symptoms are deceiving: Gonorrhea is anything but benign. If untreated, it can spread through the reproductive organs, seriously damaging tubes and ovaries. During pregnancy, gonorrhea can cause premature rupture of the membranes surrounding the fetus and premature birth. Many babies born to women with active cases of gonorrhea are blind. If you suspect that you have been exposed to gonorrhea, or if you have experienced any of the symptoms just described, tell your doctor so you can be tested. Gonorrhea is curable, and once the disease is under control, it is possible to go on and have a normal, healthy baby.

3. *Mycoplasmosis:* Very little is known about mycoplasmosis except that it may cause premature birth and the premature rupture of membranes. Unfortunately, there are no symptoms, but a doctor may consider mycoplasmosis in the

case of a patient who has had recurrent miscarriages or still-births. Once diagnosed, the problem can be treated with antibiotics.

Other Sexually Transmitted Diseases (Non-PIDS)

1. Acquired Immune Deficiency Syndrome (AIDS): AIDS is an incurable disease caused by the Human Immunodeficiency Virus, or HIV virus, that is spread through the exchange of two bodily fluids, blood and semen. Women can contract AIDS from an infected sex partner or by sharing needles with an infected person. In rare cases, AIDS has been passed through blood transfusion. I advise patients who are likely to need blood to encourage their friends or family members to donate on their behalf. Speak to your doctor about directed blood donations. Any woman who suspects that she has been exposed to AIDS should see her doctor for a blood test to determine if she has developed antibodies to the virus. A positive test result means that she has been exposed to AIDS and is at risk of developing the disease. An infected mother can pass AIDS on to her baby during childbirth or through breast-feeding.

2. *Syphilis:* Due to the widespread availability of testing procedures, syphilis is becoming a rare disease in the United States. Not so in other countries. This STD is the number one killer of infants in developing nations, and because it is still a threat to some less affluent groups in the United States, I feel it is worth a mention in this book. Syphilis, which can be successfully treated with antibiotics, progresses in three stages. During the first stage, sores appear in the genital area or on the mouth. If the disease is untreated and allowed to progress to the second stage, a rash may appear anywhere on the body, possibly accompanied by a sore throat and runny eyes. In the third and most deadly stage, the disease attacks the heart, brain, and eyes. If an expectant mother is infected with syphilis, her baby stands a 50 percent chance of dying before birth, and even if he lives, he will be born with this deadly illness. In the United States, pregnant women are routinely screened for

syphilis during their first prenatal visit. In some high-risk populations, screening may be done a second time later in pregnancy.

R—Rubella   If contracted by a mother-to-be in the first trimester, rubella or German measles can cause serious fetal
damage, including heart malformations, deafness, and mental
retardation. Before pregnancy, your doctor can order a blood
screening test to determine if you are immune to rubella. If
not, a safe and effective vaccine is available, but it should be
administered at least sixty days prior to attempting to get pregnant, since it may have a harmful affect on the fetus.

C—Cytomegalovirus or CMV   This rare virus, which can be
contracted through sexual contact as well as other means, is
especially lethal, since it can cross the placenta during pregnancy and harm the baby. Many women experience no symptoms, although some may have a mildly itchy discharge. If you
have had this virus in the past, make sure you are clear of it
before becoming pregnant. Throughout pregnancy, be careful
to monitor yourself for any change in vaginal discharge.

H—Herpes Virus 2   Herpes virus 2 is a sexually transmitted
disease that can result in miscarriage, premature labor, and
even infant death. Herpes is characterized by tiny but painful
ulcers or lesions in the vaginal and rectal area, or on the mouth.
Some people may experience flulike symptoms for a couple of
days. Although there is no cure, medication may be used to
relieve some of the symptoms. After the initial herpes attack,
the signs and symptoms of the virus may disappear, but the
virus lies dormant within the body, ready to strike at any time.
If it does reoccur, very often there are no symptoms. Although
the herpes virus rarely crosses the placenta to the fetus, it may
be contracted by the fetus if the protective membranes rupture prematurely, or during delivery when the infant passes
through the genital tract. When the virus is passed on to the
infant, it often results in death. If an expectant mother has an
active case of herpes, a cesarean delivery must be performed
to prevent the baby from contracting the virus during the
normal birth process. If you have a history of herpes, it is

critical that you notify your doctor prior to pregnancy or as soon as pregnancy is diagnosed so he can test you periodically for the virus.

TOXEMIA OR PREECLAMPSIA

Toxemia, also known as preeclampsia, or pregnancy-induced hypertension (PIH), is characterized by high blood pressure, excessive swelling, and protein in the urine, indicating a kidney malfunction. If it is not caught in its earliest stage—preeclampsia—it could lead to eclampsia, an extreme condition characterized by convulsions, coma, failure of various organ systems, and even death.

Toxemia, which usually strikes in first pregnancies, rarely appears in subsequent ones.

Any woman who has had a diagnosis of preeclampsia or toxemia in a previous pregnancy is at greater risk of miscarriage and premature birth. The problem has less to do with toxemia than with the fact that medicine is an imprecise art. What appeared to have been the symptoms of toxemia in an earlier pregnancy could have been any number of serious conditions, such as kidney malfunction or hypertension. These problems could reappear in another pregnancy. Therefore, any woman who has been diagnosed as having toxemia in a past pregnancy should be carefully monitored for recurring symptoms that could have masqueraded as toxemia in prior pregnancies.

HYPERTENSION

Women with high blood pressure who become pregnant must be closely watched by their physicians. For one thing, some medications given to normalize blood pressure, like inderol (propranolol), can be dangerous to the fetus. Fortunately, there are other drugs, like aldomet (methyldopa), that have proved to be safe for expectant mothers. Therefore, it's critical that hypertensive women consult with their doctors before becoming pregnant.

DO NOT STOP TAKING MEDICATION FOR HYPERTENSION WITHOUT CONSULTING YOUR DOCTOR. If unchecked, high blood pressure can pose serious problems to both mother and fetus.

The combination of hypertension and the added stress of pregnancy can result in impaired brain, kidney, and heart function. At the same time, poor circulation to the uterus and placenta—a direct result of hypertension—can result in an oxygen-deprived, malnourished fetus. Consequently, women with high blood pressure are at risk of premature birth and low-birth-weight babies.

About 7 percent of all pregnant women develop high blood pressure, or preeclampsia, during pregnancy. If a woman is at risk of hypertension—that is, if she's overweight, diabetic, over age thirty-five, or has a family history of the disorder—she should be especially vigilant about monitoring her blood pressure.

Although hypertension can pose serious risks in a pregnancy, these problems are not insurmountable. Far from it. If properly managed, most of these mothers-to-be can have uneventful pregnancies and normal, healthy babies. The key is alerting your doctor to the condition prior to pregnancy, or if already pregnant, catching it early on before it can do any damage. Self-monitoring of your blood pressure may help reduce the risk and enhance your pregnancy.

DIABETES

Diabetes is characterized by too much glucose or sugar in the blood. The condition is caused by the body's inability to make enough insulin, a hormone produced by the pancreas that controls the levels of carbohydrates and amino acids in the system. When the body fails to make enough insulin, or when the hormone is not being used properly, the blood glucose level becomes too high and many metabolic problems can arise.

Some people develop diabetes during childhood, others become diabetic as they get older. As a result of hormonal changes, some pregnant women develop a condition called gestational diabetes. In fact, gestational diabetes is the most common medical complication of pregnancy, affecting about 10 percent of all pregnancies. Women with an immediate relative—such as a mother, sister, or aunt—with diabetes are at greater risk. Whether the diabetes was a preexisting condition or was triggered by pregnancy makes very little difference—it can pose a serious threat to both mother and child.

Diabetic mothers are at risk of preeclampsia, and are also prone to urinary tract infections, which, if untreated, can spread from the bladder to the kidneys, hampering kidney function. There is also a higher risk of stillbirth and birth defects among diabetics.

Other problems that can develop include macrosomia, a condition that causes abnormally large fetal growth; respiratory distress syndrome (RDS), which can severely affect the baby's ability to breathe after birth; and polyhydramnios, too much amniotic fluid in the sac surrounding the fetus, impairing the ability of the mother to breathe. In addition, diabetes may cause premature labor, abnormal positioning of the baby, and labor complications.

Because of these and other possible problems, diabetics are at greater risk of miscarriage and premature labor. If complications arise, a diabetic may be forced to deliver her baby earlier than term.

On the bright side, most women can control diabetes through dietary modification. In some cases, shots of insulin are prescribed throughout pregnancy. Thanks to home monitoring kits that make it possible for women to measure blood glucose levels on their own, most diabetics need not be hospitalized during pregnancy.

The list of things that can go wrong may be scary to diabetic women who are contemplating pregnancy. So let me offer these words of comfort. In my practice, I have found that diabetic women who take good care of themselves and are active participants in their pregnancies stand as good a chance as anyone else of having a normal, healthy baby. With proper medical care, what can go wrong usually doesn't, and the overwhelming majority of these pregnancies are extremely successful.

A HISTORY OF ECTOPIC OR TUBAL PREGNANCIES

An ectopic pregnancy results when the fertilized egg never reaches the womb, but lodges outside of the uterus, either on the abdomen or an ovary or, in the case of the most common type of ectopic pregnancy, right in the fallopian tube. If uninterrupted, the tubal pregnancy will eventually erupt in the tube, threatening the life of the mother. No one knows why this happens, or why some women are more prone to it than others. Women who have had numerous sexual partners, or who were IUD users, may be at risk of ectopic pregnancy, since they may have suffered from more low-grade infections that resulted in tubal scarring.

A woman who has already had one ectopic pregnancy should be especially vigilant in early pregnancy, watching for signs of a second, typically abdominal pain and vaginal bleeding, and in some cases, shoulder pain. Alerted to the problem, her doctor will perform an early pregnancy test and order an ultrasound—a noninvasive procedure that allows him to look inside the womb—to determine whether the pregnancy is developing where it should—inside the uterus.

If an ectopic pregnancy is discovered, the pregnancy usually must be removed surgically, although in rare cases, nonsurgical treatment may be possible. In many, but not all cases, the fallopian tube may be saved.

When DES Daughters Become Mothers

In the 1950s, DES (diethylstilbestrol), a synthetic estrogenlike hormone, was given to pregnant women to prevent miscarriage. To this day, doctors disagree as to whether or not the hormone treatment was effective. While some may feel that it prevented miscarriages, others feel that the drug may have had a "placebo effect" on the women who took it. I believe that it is also possible that many of these women carried to term because their doctors were more attentive and more likely to intervene at critical points in the pregnancy.

Whatever the reason, more than one million of the women who took DES successfully carried pregnancies to term. In the late 1960s, a rare cancer, clear cell adenocarcinoma, was found in some of the daughters of mothers who took DES. This discovery generated a great deal of anxiety on the part of DES mothers and their children, since at the time, no one knew how many of these children would contract the cancer. Today we know that only one out of 10,000 DES babies will get this kind of cancer. We also know that if it's detected early, it can be successfully treated.

Although most DES-exposed children will never get cancer, ironically, many are plagued by the very problem the drug was meant to prevent—miscarriage and premature labor. Many DES daughters were born with structural abnormalities in their reproductive tract, including malformation of the fallopian tubes and uterus, an unusually shaped uterus, and a weakened cervix. All of these problems can make it difficult for these women to conceive and sustain a pregnancy.

Fortunately, with proper planning, most of the problems can be overcome. It is critical that an obstetrician know ahead of time that a patient might have been exposed to DES in utero so he can closely monitor the pregnancy. Pelvic exams, which are not normally performed during pregnancy except at the very beginning and end, must be done more frequently for these women to detect signs of a weakened cervix and other abnormalities. If your physician is not experienced with DES patients, you can provide him with information from such organizations as DES Action, which offers a comprehensive guide to handling these pregnancies (see the appendix for further information).

Although pregnancy for DES-exposed women does pose a special risk, with good planning and proper medical care, the odds are in their favor.

The Rh Factor: When Opposites Attract

The Rh factor refers to a type of protein found on the red blood cells. Most people, including 85 percent of all women, are Rh positive. A minority of people do not have this Rh factor and are called Rh negative. A quick and simple lab test reveals whether you are Rh positive or Rh negative.

While the Rh factor has no effect on health, in certain instances it can wreak havoc on a pregnancy. A dangerous situation can arise if an Rh negative woman and an Rh positive man produce an Rh positive child. (There's no problem if her husband is also Rh negative.) Here's why. When an Rh negative person comes in contact with Rh positive blood, she becomes sensitized. That is, the mother begins to produce antibodies to fight off the foreign substance. If she is carrying a baby who has inherited the father's Rh positive protein, the mother's protective antibodies could cross the placenta, where they would wage war on the fetal red blood cells. Depending on the severity of the situation, the fetus could develop a mild to serious anemia. Severe anemia may lead to stillbirth.

The Rh factor rarely poses a problem in a first pregnancy, since it is unlikely that isoimmunization would occur, that is, that the maternal and fetal blood supplies would mingle, causing the mother to produce the dangerous antibodies. However, during labor and delivery the barriers between the infant and the maternal circulatory systems begin to break down, increasing the likelihood of an exchange of blood. Once exposed to the Rh positive blood, the mother would begin producing the antibodies. These same antibodies could attack the fetal blood cells in subsequent pregnancies.

If I had been writing this book at a time when your mothers were having children, I could have offered little hope to Rh negative women who were contemplating second pregnancies with Rh positive husbands. Today, with proper management, it makes no difference whether opposites—or negatives—attract. At the first sign of pregnancy, doctors routinely screen patients to determine blood type. If a patient tests Rh negative, and her husband tests Rh positive, the doctor typically orders further testing to see if she has already developed antibodies to Rh positive blood. If she hasn't, her doctor may give her Rh immune globulin (RhIG), a blood product that can prevent the production of these potentially harmful antibodies. RhIG is usually given around the twenty-eighth week of pregnancy and after the birth if the child is Rh positive. RhIG must be administered after each pregnancy involving an Rh positive child, as well as after an ectopic or tubal pregnancy, miscarriage, induced abortion, amniocentesis, or any other event in which maternal and fetal blood may have been exchanged, in order to further reduce the risk of this problem.

What if the Rh negative mother has already developed the harmful antibodies? The fetus must be closely watched for signs of anemia. In the more severe—and thankfully, very rare cases—the fetus may require a blood transfusion in utero to replace the diseased blood cells. Through ultrasound guidance, the physician places a needle through the mother's abdomen into the umbilical cord. Good blood is then administered to the ailing baby. In competent hands, this procedure is fairly safe and usually quite successful. However, in some cases, if the fetus is seriously ill, it may be necessary to induce birth earlier than normal so he can receive immediate care.

A-B-O Incompatibility

There are four possible blood types, A, B, AB, and O. As with Rh incompatibility, a possible problem could exist if a mother with one type of blood carries a child who has inherited a different blood type from his father. Fortunately, most mothers have no difficulty carrying a child with a different blood type to term. In a small minority of cases, however, the mother may develop antibodies to fight off the pregnancy, resulting in miscarriage.

Placental Problems

The placenta is a remarkable organ that is created solely to support the pregnancy and is expelled immediately after birth. Resembling a large, flat pie, the placenta, which weighs around 2 pounds, is linked to the fetus through the umbilical cord. At the very early stages of conception, the fertilized egg, after two divisions, differentiates into two portions, one destined to become the embryo, and the other, the placenta.

The placenta has many functions. Vital nutrients and oxygen flow from the placenta through the umbilical cord to the fetus in one direction, while carbon dioxide and fetal waste flow in another. While the fetus is living in the uterus, the placenta performs the functions that will be taken over by the lungs, stomach, intestines, and kidneys after birth.

This multifaceted organ also functions as a gland, producing vital hormones to sustain the pregnancy, such as estrogen, progesterone, and chorionic gonadotropin.

If the placenta is impaired in any way, the survival of the fetus may be seriously threatened. However, as you will see later in this book, if a problem is detected early, much can be done to improve placental performance.

The following is a list of some of the more common placental problems.

1. *Placenta Previa:*   This potentially life-threatening situation occurs when the placenta grows over all or part of the cervix. In a normal pregnancy, the fertilized egg should implant on the upper portion of the womb. In some cases, however, the implant occurs in the lower portion. Consequently, the placenta covers the cervix, the mouth of the womb. In the case of a complete coverage, these babies must be delivered by cesarean section. In severe cases, however, placenta previa can result in serious internal hemorrhaging and fetal loss. Painless bleeding is often an early warning sign of placenta previa.

2. *Abruptio Placentae:*   The placenta separates from the uterine wall, which depending on the severity of the condition and stage of the pregnancy, could cause miscarriage, premature birth, or fetal death. Bleeding, abdominal pain, and a sudden drop in blood pressure are some of the symptoms.

3. *Malfunctioning Placenta:*   For a variety of possible reasons, the placenta ceases to provide adequate nutrients to the fetus. A maternal illness, such as preeclampsia, could be causing poor circulation to the uterus, or an infection could have attacked the placenta, preventing it from functioning properly. Blood clots in the placenta could be interfering with the transport of materials to and from the fetus. In rare cases, the problem could be a rapidly aging placenta—that is, for some mysterious reason, the placenta is ready to throw in the towel before its job is completed.

The only symptoms of a malfunctioning placenta would be a smaller than normal baby for gestational age, or a decline in fetal activity.

Uterine Abnormalities

About ten days after conception, the fertilized egg completes its journey from the fallopian tube to the uterus, where it embeds in the uterine wall in a process called nidation. The new life will grow within the uterus until the baby is ready to live independently outside of the mother. However, if the uterus fails to provide an ideal environment for the developing baby, problems can arise, resulting in miscarriage and premature birth. The following are some common uterine abnormalities that can interfere with your ability to carry to term.

Uterine Fibroids

About 5 percent of all white and 10 percent of all black women develop uterine fibroids, benign uterine muscle growths. While fibroids can be harmless, especially if they develop late in life, they can pose a serious threat to a pregnancy. In the worst-case scenario, the placenta and fertilized egg attach onto the fibroid instead of directly onto the uterine wall. Unable to develop properly, the pregnancy will end in miscarriage.

Even if the placenta and fertilized egg manage to circumvent the growths and attach securely to the uterine wall, the problems are far from over. Due to the high estrogen and progesterone levels of pregnancy, the fibroids may become enlarged. If they become too big, the uterus may start to contract and that, in turn, could result in miscarriage and premature labor. In rare cases, the fibroids may block the birth canal, necessitating a cesarean section, or they may grow so big that they press against the baby, causing compression deformity.

Although some women with fibroids may carry to term

with few problems, if you know you have fibroids, it's a good idea to talk to your physician before becoming pregnant. Through careful examination, including an ultrasound and a hysterosalpingogram (X ray of the uterus and tubes), he can determine the likelihood of the fibroids causing difficulty during pregnancy. In some cases, a surgical procedure called a myomectomy, or removal of the fibroid tumors while keeping the uterus intact, may be recommended.

Misshaped Uterus

A normal uterus or womb is triangular-shaped. If there is any deviation in that shape, it could pose a problem during pregnancy. For example, women who were exposed to DES in utero typically have a T-shaped uterus. (See the section "When DES Daughters Become Mothers" earlier in this chapter.)

If the pregnancy lodges in a part of the uterus where it cannot grow properly, the uterus will push it out, thus causing a miscarriage. Another case in point is that of the heart-shaped uterus. As in the case of the T-shaped uterus, the pregnancy cannot survive if it selects the wrong location.

Defects in uterine shape can be diagnosed by using hysterosalpingogram; hysteroscopy, a procedure in which a small, pencil-shaped instrument with a light is inserted in the cervix, enabling the physician to look inside the uterus; or through ultrasound. Although it may be difficult to detect without these procedures, uterine abnormality may be suspected if a patient has a history of recurring urinary tract infection or repeat miscarriages.

Asherman's Syndrome

This condition is characterized by adhesions inside the uterus, caused by excessive scraping during a D and C done after a miscarriage or previous abortion. It may also occur as a result of infection.

Incompetent Cervix

The cervix is an opening located at the mouth of the womb. During pregnancy, the cervix must stay tightly closed to support the growing fetus. In some cases, the cervix may have been weakened due to previous miscarriage, premature labor, abortion, or D and C. However, some women may be born with a weak cervix. If there is a cervical weakness, when the uterus expands and the growing fetus presses down on the cervix, the cervix gives way, resulting in miscarriage or premature birth. The cervical, or mucus, plugs—the layer of mucus inside the cervix that protects the uterus from bacteria or other foreign particles—may begin to drip down into the vagina. A mucousy discharge the consistency of an egg white is one symptom of an incompetent cervix that may be present in early pregnancy. As the pregnancy progresses, women with this problem may feel pressure in the pelvic area, menstrual-type cramps, or lower-back ache. However, some women may not experience any symptoms, or the symptoms may be very subtle. Since this condition can be very serious, even the slightest symptom should not be ignored.

Retroverted or Tilted Uterus

About 30 percent of all women have retroverted or backward-tilted uteruses, which lean toward the rectum instead of the front of the abdomen. Usually, this is not a serious problem, since the uterus often falls into place by itself in early pregnancy.

In some of these cases, however, the uterus stays put. As the uterus enlarges to accommodate the growing fetus, the uterus pushes into the back. Eventually, it will run out of room to grow and the fetus may be forced out in premature labor.

Although this doesn't happen often, it's important for both doctor and mother-to-be to be aware of the potential problem. Early in pregnancy, a doctor may advise a patient with a tilted uterus to sleep on her stomach in an attempt to tilt it forward. The doctor may also help tilt it forward during an examination.

If all else fails, he may insert a special device called a pessary into the vagina to help eliminate the backward tilt.

While I don't want to throw every woman with a backward-tilted uterus into a panic, I do believe it is important to understand that if it doesn't correct itself, it can create special problems. I have seen enough women coming to me after having miscarried because of this problem—a problem I feel could have been easily corrected if it had been addressed early in the pregnancies.

Weakened Cervix Because of Previous Cervical Cone Biopsy

A cervical cone biopsy is a surgical procedure in which a small portion of the cervix is removed. It may be performed on a woman who is suspected of having cancer, in which case the removed tissue would be examined for any abnormal cell growth, or it may also be performed to remove a known cancerous growth. Whatever the reason for the cervical cone biopsy, the procedure can result in a weakened cervix that puts the mother-to-be at greater risk of miscarriage and premature birth.

Immunological Disorders

When a foreign tissue is introduced into the body, as in the case of a heart or kidney transplant, the body begins to produce antibodies and white blood cells to fight off the intruder. This process is called an immunological rejection. Without the aid of strong medications to suppress this reaction, the new organs would be rejected.

This immunological response may play a role in miscarriage. In the 1950s, Peter Medawar, a Nobel Prize–winning scientist who was researching methods of tissue implantation raised an interesting question: "How does the pregnant mother contrive to nourish within herself, for many weeks or months, a fetus which is an antigenically foreign body?" Or in plain English, Medawar was asking, "Why doesn't an expectant mother reject a fetus—which is after all, a foreign substance—the way an organ transplant patient would reject a donated organ?"

Some immunologists believe that in a normal pregnancy, the mother's immune system is somehow suppressed to prevent the immunological rejection caused by the harmful antibodies and white blood cells. In fact, some theorize that the fetal-placental unit produces a substance called "blocking factor," an antibody that prevents the mother's white blood cells from rejecting the child's tissues.

However, some doctors believe that in some rare cases, women may be carrying pregnancies that do not produce this blocking factor, or lack other mechanisms that may suppress the mother's immune system. Therefore, the mother produces antibodies and white blood cells that attack the fetus and the placenta, resulting in miscarriage.

There are no symptoms other than the fact that a woman may have several unexplained miscarriages. The immune theory of miscarriage is controversial and not widely accepted by doctors. Nevertheless, I feel it should be considered in cases of recurrent miscarriage where all other possibilities have been ruled out.

Another small group of women who have suffered from chronic miscarriages may have an actual disease of the immune system called the antiphospholipid antibody syndrome. In this disease, the immune system, which is supposed to protect against outside invaders, begins to turn against its own body.

Phospholipids are chemicals that make up the membranes of virtually all body cells. People with antiphospholipid antibody syndrome produce antibodies that attack phospholipids. During pregnancy, these antibodies may attack the placenta, resulting in starvation of the fetus and eventual miscarriage.

Some but not all women with this syndrome may be prone to thrombosis or blood clots. However, the only manifestation of this disease may be the mother's inability to carry a pregnancy to term.

Since this disease typically strikes between ages twenty and forty, a woman may have carried a pregnancy to term before developing this syndrome. However, women with a tendency to develop this disease may have encountered complications in previous pregnancies, including hypertension, or may have given birth to babies that were small for their gestational age.

If a doctor suspects a patient has this disease, he can perform a blood test to verify the presence of the antiphospholipid antibodies.

Treatment for immunological disorders as well as other causes of miscarriage and premature labor is discussed in detail in chapter 9, "New Hope for Problem Pregnancies."

TWO

Genetics and Your Pregnancy

If you haven't thought about genetics since your high school biology teacher ruined a promising lecture on reproduction by talking about pea plants and fruit flies, it's time to brush up on the basics.

Genetic abnormalities are responsible for a significant number of miscarriages, especially in the first trimester. Every couple contemplating pregnancy should fully understand the profound role genetics will play in the health and well-being of their baby.

Genetics is the study of the science of heredity. Just as we have inherited certain traits and characteristics from our parents, we, in turn, will pass on certain traits and characteristics to our offspring. Biological traits, such as height, hair color, body type and even the predisposition to develop certain diseases are passed down from generation to generation through the process of reproduction.

When a woman's egg cell unites with a man's sperm cell, each contributes 23 single chromosomes to create a new cell with the requisite 23 pairs or 46 total. Chromosomes are tiny, rodlike structures inside the nucleus of every body cell. Each chromosome consists of thousands of genes, which are chemicals that store information. There are 100,000 genes in total, and each one determines a different trait or characteristic.

Within these chromosomes lies the blueprint for the new life. At the moment of fertilization, the child's sex is determined by the father, who either donates an X or a Y chromosome to match the mother's X chromosome. If the child is an XX, it is a girl. If it is an XY, it is a boy.

Each parent contributes an equal number of genes to the offspring, but all genes are not created equal. Dominant genes take precedence over recessive genes. For example, in the case of eye color, the gene for brown eyes is dominant over the gene for blue. If a brown-eyed mother donates her brown gene to the offspring, it will dominate over any recessive blue gene donated by the father. However, the child will now carry one dominant brown gene and one recessive blue. Let's say the child grows up and marries someone who also carries a dominant brown and a recessive blue. They have a 25 percent chance of producing a blue-eyed child who will inherit both recessive blue genes, a 50 percent chance of producing a brown-eyed child with one dominant brown and one recessive blue gene, and a 25 percent chance of having a brown-eyed child with two brown genes.

Although most genes are normal, everyone carries a certain number of defective or potentially harmful genes. Fortunately, healthy genes usually dominate over faulty ones, but not always. There are some abnormal genes that are dominant, as in the case of the gene for Huntington's chorea, a degenerative disorder of the nervous system. If a parent is carrying the single dominant abnormal gene for Huntington's chorea, he has a 50 percent chance of passing the disorder on to his child.

There is always a risk that two carriers of the same recessive defective gene will unite and pass the problem on to their offspring. For instance, about one in twenty-five American Jews of European descent carry a recessive gene for Tay-Sachs disease, a lethal biochemical disorder. In fact, the vast majority of these people don't even know that they're carriers, since they themselves are not affected nor probably are any of their close relatives. If a Tay-Sachs carrier has a child with a noncarrier, the child will be healthy. A problem arises, however, if a carrier bears a child with another carrier. Since the Tay-Sachs gene is recessive—like the gene for blue eyes we discussed earlier—the likelihood of producing a child with the disorder is about 25 percent. There is a simple blood test that can determine whether or not someone is a carrier of the Tay-Sachs gene, and most doctors recommend it for their Jewish patients. The test, however, should be done before a woman gets pregnant, since pregnancy hormones can interfere with the accuracy of the result.

Some defective genes are carried solely on the sex chromosomes. For instance, the gene for hemophilia—a disease characterized by uncontrollable bleeding—is carried on one of the maternal X chromosomes. If the mother has a daughter, she will be normal because the father's X chromosome will cancel out the bad gene. However, if the mother has a son—which means that there is no healthy X gene from the father to counteract the faulty one—he has a 50 percent chance of inheriting her gene for hemophilia.

Some genetic defects are caused by an abnormal number of chromosomes. For example, children born with Down's syndrome, once known as mongolism, have 47 instead of the normal 46 chromosomes. The extra chromosome is located on the twenty-first pair, resulting in trisomy 21, Down's syndrome. This condition is characterized by mental retardation and is often accompanied by physical abnormalities that can be life-threatening. (Trisomies involving other chromosomes can produce similar birth defects.)

No one knows for sure why this happens, but some scientists speculate that the problem may originate in the ovaries where the egg cells or ova are produced. The female ova starts out with 46 chromosomes. Before it can be united with the sperm, however, it needs to shed 23 single-stranded chromosomes so the newly formed cell will have the requisite 46 in the correct alignment of 23 pairs. In a process called meiosis that takes place only in the reproductive tissue, the egg cell or ovum divides, forming a new cell with 23 chromosomes and a duplicate cell called a polar body, which will eventually disintegrate. Some researchers believe that during meiosis the eggs produced by older mothers may be more prone to genetic aberration than those produced by younger ones. For example, the older mother may be more likely to produce an egg cell with an extra chromosome, or one that is missing a chromosome. Other theories suggest that during the process of fertilization, some of the chromosomes donated by older mothers and fathers may stick together inappropriately, lining up incorrectly in the newly formed cell.

Although older mothers may be more prone to chromosomal aberrations, genetic defects can happen to anyone. In the early stages of conception, when the fertilized egg begins the process of mitosis or cell division, a lot can go wrong. A chromosome may be dropped accidentally, or an extra chromosome may be picked up. The genes that belong on one chromosome may end up on another. Any deviation in the lineup of the standard 23 pairs may cause a genetic defect. To understand why this happens, think of the 46 chromosomes as 23 chapters in a massive textbook describing the complicated process of building a human being. Now think of each gene as a page in this great book. If the chapters and pages are out of sequence, the result is likely to be very confusing. Thus, when the chromosomes and genes somehow get scrambled during replication, the information they are trying to transmit cannot be deciphered properly by the cells that are creating the new life.

Most unions resulting in genetic abnormalities end in spontaneous abortion. However, Mother Nature is not infallible, and some of these defective eggs are carried to term.

About 1 percent of all couples will have a child with a serious, life-threatening birth defect. As we discussed earlier, the risk of having a child with a serious chromosomal abnormality increases as the mother ages. For example, at age twenty, a woman has about a 1:2,000 chance of having a baby with Down's syndrome and about a 1:526 risk of bearing a child with a significant chromosomal abnormality. However, at age thirty-five, a woman has about a 1:300 chance of having a Down's baby, and her risk of having a child with a significant chromosomal abnormality is about 1:179. By age forty, the odds shift dramatically. A woman now has about a 1:100 risk of having a child with Down's syndrome, and a 1:63 chance of having a child with a serious chromosomal defect. (Fortunately, many of these chromosomal abnormalities can be detected in pregnancy, and we talk about these testing procedures in chapter 8, "Inside the Womb: Keeping Track of Your Baby from Conception to Birth.")

Unions resulting in chromosomal abnormalities are responsible for a sizable number of spontaneous abortions in the first trimester. In the first half of the first trimester, about 60 percent of all spontaneous abortions or miscarriages are caused by genetic defects. During the second half of the first trimester, these abnormalities are responsible for about 15 to 20 percent of all miscarriages. In the second trimester, however, only 10 percent of all miscarriages can be attributed to genetic problems.

Studies show that people who have miscarried two times or more have a higher rate of chromosomal abnormalities than the general population. For instance, in about 6 percent of all couples with a history of multiple miscarriages, one or both parents have a genetic defect known as a balanced translocation or a rearrangement of the chromosomal material. In these cases, unlike that of an extra chromosome, the total amount of genetic material is normal, but it is incorrectly arranged. While the parent may be perfectly normal, the genetic code he is passing on to his offspring is not. It is possible, however, depending on how the translocation behaves during reproduction, for the parent to have a healthy baby.

A doctor might recommend that a couple who has miscarried more than once undergo a karyotype, or a chromosomal evaluation. Blood is taken from both parents. Through special staining techniques, the chromosomes within the cell nuclei are identified and analyzed for any translocations or other abnormalities. While we're still not able to correct any chromosomal defects, we are often able to assess the couple's likelihood of bearing a normal child. Based on this information, the couple can then decide how they want to proceed.

Genetic Counseling:
What It Is and Who Needs It

A genetic counselor is someone who can provide expert advice on the different types of chromosomal abnormalities and genetic disorders, and can help a couple assess the likelihood of passing a particular genetic problem on to their offspring.

Genetic counseling is not for everyone. Some couples, even if they are at risk of passing a genetic disorder to their offspring, do not want or need this information. They are willing to brave the odds and accept whatever child comes their way. That is their right.

However, there are many other couples who want and need this information, but don't know where to get it, or are reluctant to seek it out.

"The term 'counseling' turns some people off," notes Joan Kegerize, a genetic counselor to whom I frequently refer patients. "Many patients think that seeing a genetic counselor is like seeing a psychologist, that somehow, our purpose is to psychoanalyze them. Others are afraid that we're going to try to push them in one direction or another. For instance, if they're against abortion, they may be afraid that we're going to urge them to have one. Or, if they have a genetic problem in their family, they may be worried that we'll tell them they shouldn't have kids. That's not what a genetic counselor does. Our job is to help people make their own decisions by providing information and education."

Ideally, couples who have reason to be worried about bearing a child with a chromosomal abnormality should seek counseling before pregnancy. I have seen patients spend months needlessly worrying about the possibility of a genetic problem only to learn that their fears were unfounded. Consider the case of Mary Ann, two months pregnant when she told me that her father had a son from a previous marriage who was so severely retarded that he had been institutionalized shortly after birth. To complicate matters further, her father was unaware of the cause of the retardation. Naturally, Mary Ann was very concerned that the condition might somehow run in her family. As much as I wanted to relieve her anxieties, I told her

I needed to know the specifics of her brother's case before I could offer any advice.

This was easier said than done. First, Mary Ann's father, a noncustodial parent, had to get his ex-wife to sign a consent form releasing their son's medical records. Since the son had been hospitalized several times outside of the institution, his doctor had to write to the hospital to arrange to get copies of the young man's medical records. The entire process took close to two months, during which time Mary Ann was growing more nervous with each passing day.

It wasn't until Mary Ann was well into her second trimester that we learned that her brother's problem was not caused by a genetic abnormality but by a medical complication following a premature delivery. Greatly relieved, Mary Ann finally began to enjoy the remaining months of her pregnancy. Think of the stress Mary Ann could have been spared had she only sought out this information before getting pregnant!

Mary Ann was lucky to learn that her brother's condition was not hereditary. But what if the report had been just the opposite? What if, at nearly five months pregnant, Mary Ann was told that there was some chromosomal abnormality lurking in her family that could strike future generations? Some might argue that it would be cruel to give this information to a woman who has already completed half her pregnancy. Others may feel that this knowledge might push someone into aborting a possibly healthy fetus. Therefore, the conclusion they would draw is that genetic counseling should be avoided.

As a patients' rights advocate, however, I believe patients have a right to know as much as they want—and that means bad news as well as good. They also need to be informed about their options.

In Mary Ann's case, a genetic counselor could provide information on the specific disorder affecting her brother—and, more importantly, the likelihood of it happening again—so that Mary Ann and her husband could draw their own conclusions. If Mary Ann wanted to be certain whether or not her baby would be affected, she and the counselor could discuss the possibility of genetic evaluation of the offspring, such as amniocentesis.

If Mary Ann had later learned that her child was going to suffer from mental retardation, she and her husband could have then decided how they wanted to proceed. Abortion is one option, but there are many others. Even before the child was born, Mary Ann and her husband could have investigated special schools and programs for mentally disabled children in their area, and they could also have linked up with other parents who were facing the challenge of raising children with special needs.

By the time the child was born, I believe they would have been better able to cope with the situation.

The decision to seek genetic counseling is ultimately one you will make jointly with your partner and your doctor. I feel, however, that anyone who falls into the following risk groups should give the matter careful consideration.

1. *History of Chromosomal Abnormality:* If either you or your spouse knows of any chromosomal abnormality in your family, such as a close relative with Down's syndrome—or if you suspect that there might be one—counseling can be helpful to determine your risks of having a child with a similar problem.

2. *Known or Suspected Carrier Parents:* Since people of the same race, nationality, and religion often end up married to each other, the gene for certain disorders may be more prevalent among some ethnic groups than others. For instance, people of Mediterranean, South Asian, or African ancestry are more likely to be carriers of the thalassemia trait. Thalassemia refers to a broad range of disorders that produce anemia, a deficiency of red blood cells. Some forms of thalassemia are quite benign, while others, such as Cooley's anemia, can be life-threatening. The thalassemia trait can be detected through a simple blood test.

There are many other examples of genetic disorders that affect specific populations. The gene for sickle-cell anemia, another inherited blood disease, is carried by 1 in 10 American blacks. Sickle-cell anemia is characterized by an abnormally shaped red blood cell that resembles a crescent or a sickle.

There is no cure for this painful and life-threatening condition. Fortunately, carriers can be detected through a simple blood screening test. If necessary, amniocentesis can be performed at about sixteen weeks' gestation to determine if two carriers have passed this serious illness on to their offspring.

Since it takes two carriers of a recessive gene disorder to pass the disorder to future generations, much of the worry can be eliminated if one, or, if need be, both members of the couple undergo testing before pregnancy. In this case, genetic counseling can be very useful and can eliminate a great deal of anguish later on.

3. *Maternal and Paternal Age:* If the mother is thirty-five or older, or the father is over fifty-five, a genetic counselor can help explain the risks of pregnancy as well as describe the various prenatal tests available to screen for specific genetic disorders.

4. *Repeated Fetal Loss:* Any couple who has experienced two or more unexplained miscarriages or stillbirths should seek a genetic evaluation.

5. *Teratogen Exposure:* A teratogen is any agent that can induce or increase the incidence of birth defects. At one time, it was believed that the placenta acted as a barrier, shielding the fetus from any undesirable substances consumed by the mother. Now we know that many substances can pass from the mother to the fetus via the placenta.

A teratogen can be a drug, as in the case of thalidomide, a sedative used in the 1950s that produced malformation of the limbs of children exposed in utero. Or a teratogen can be an infection, such as the rubella virus, known for causing severe congenital heart defects, deafness, cataracts, and other problems. A teratogen can also be the radiation emitted by an X-ray machine, or perhaps even the rays given off by a video display terminal (VDT), recently implicated as a possible cause of miscarriage.

The list of known teratogens is fairly short, but the list of suspected teratogens is growing each day as we are forced to live in a world that is plagued by pollution, questionable food additives, and toxic waste. If you're planning on becoming pregnant, your best bet is to avoid all known teratogens and if possible, to limit your exposure to suspected ones. If you are exposed to a teratogenic substance, especially in early pregnancy, genetic counseling is recommended.

THREE

Good Conceptions: Preparing for Pregnancy

Starting Over: A Game Plan for Success

My husband and I were thirty-five. Our daughter was ten and our son was eight. Our desire for another child was growing stronger. After all, time was running out. I had no difficulty conceiving or carrying my previous pregnancies. When we made the decision to have another child, we expected it to be smooth sailing. Within two months, I was pregnant and we were thrilled. It was going to be great. At ten weeks, the cramps started and then the bleeding. Within two days I lost the baby and had my first D and C.

"Why did it happen?" I asked my doctor.

"It's nature's way."

Saddened, but determined, I decided to try again. Three months later, I received the good news. Test positive. Pregnant again. This time, I vowed to do things differently. I cut down on my activities and got more rest.

Yet, at eight weeks, it started all over again. The cramps, the bleeding. Another miscarriage.

"Why did it happen again?"

He shrugged. "It's nature's way."

— Nancy, mother of a two-year-old girl

*T*wo years ago, after two miscarriages within a six-month period, Nancy and her husband, Alan, came to see me to discuss whether or not they should abandon their dream of having another child. Understandably, they did not want to pursue another pregnancy unless they had a good chance of success.

Statistically, the odds were against them. After one miscarriage, a woman has a 20 to 30 percent chance of miscarrying again. A woman like Nancy who has had two previous miscarriages stands a better than 50 percent chance of losing another baby.

Before I could give Nancy and Alan a definitive answer, I needed to learn more about why they had lost the previous pregnancies. Was it "nature's way" of disposing of a defective fetus, as their doctor had suggested? Or were there other factors at work that were thwarting their efforts to have a child?

Discovering the cause of a pregnancy loss requires a great deal of detective work on the part of the doctor and the patient or couple. When it comes to detecting the cause of a miscarriage, there are no shortcuts. Unlike Dr. McCoy in "Star Trek," twentieth-century doctors like myself are unable to simply wave a scanning device over a patient's body and immediately come up with a diagnosis. Although there are literally hundreds of sophisticated tests and techniques that can aid in our diagnosis, no one medical procedure can provide a complete overview of what went wrong.

Since it would be far too costly and time-consuming to order every possible test for every patient, the physician must first narrow down the range of possibilities. Then, if the diagnosis is still unknown or unconfirmed, the appropriate tests can be performed.

Note: The first and most important step is to take a careful and complete medical history of the patient.

As in Nancy's case, many doctors assume they know their patients so well that they need not do an extensive investigation after each miscarriage. They may honestly believe that they will learn nothing new. Others may feel that it will only serve to dredge up bad memories for their patient. Still others may fear that if they do find something they overlooked, the patient will blame them for not catching it the first time.

I feel that whatever the reason, doctors who fail to perform a careful evaluation after each pregnancy loss are doing their patients a disservice. Given the fact that each miscarriage increases a woman's chances of having another, it is imperative that she begin every pregnancy from a position of strength. Before she even attempts another pregnancy, she and her doctor should do everything in their power to ensure that the next one is successful.

After each miscarriage, the doctor should do a complete review of the patient's medical history, as if she had walked into his office for the first time. Nothing should be taken for granted. This in-depth interview should include a review of the patient's past miscarriages, abortions, menstrual irregularities, illnesses, or treatments for gynecological problems that could put her at risk of miscarrying again. (See the checklist at the end of this section.)

The doctor must be careful to ask detailed questions, since a patient may not always know which facts are significant and which are not. In turn, the patient must be made to feel free to volunteer whatever information she feels is relevant. It is also important to review any symptoms that may have accompanied the miscarriage, such as pain, bleeding, or fever, which could shed some light on why it happened and on the likelihood of its happening again.

The patient history should be accompanied by a thorough physical examination to check for any signs of what could have caused the miscarriage. At least two physical exams are needed: one immediately following the loss, and one between eight and ten weeks later. (See the section later in this chapter, entitled "Gathering the Clues.")

During the post-miscarriage interview, a doctor should encourage his patient to discuss her feelings about the loss, and to raise any questions she may have. Doctors, like everyone else, may feel uncomfortable dealing with grief. It saddens me, however, when I hear many patients complain that their doctors did not even attempt to offer emotional support or understanding. In fact, many women feel that their doctors are actually disappointed in them for losing the baby. "I felt as if I had failed to do my part, and now I had to prove myself by getting 'back on the horse,' so to speak," I was told by one of my patients.

As another one of my patients put it so eloquently, "Six weeks after the miscarriage, I had many questions about why I lost the baby. I couldn't help but think that I must have done something to cause the miscarriage. I was still crying myself to sleep every night. My doctor didn't want to hear about any of this. He told me it wasn't good to 'wallow' in grief and that I should get pregnant again as soon as possible."

There's nothing wrong with encouraging a patient to pursue another pregnancy if that is what she wants. In fact, in most cases, a woman should be able to get pregnant again after two or three normal menstrual cycles. However, for some women, the emotional wounds may take longer to heal. These women may need more time to accept the loss and to gather the strength to start over. As I tell my patients, let your heart be your guide. Regardless of what anyone tells you, only you and your spouse can decide when the time is right to start another pregnancy.

Although the post-miscarriage interview can be time-consuming—it can take several hours to get a complete and accurate history and to discuss other related issues—I have found that it is well worth the effort. After a careful review of the patient's history and a thorough physical examination, I am able, about 80 percent of the time at the very least, to narrow down the list of possible culprits so I can better plan for the next pregnancy. Sometimes I am even able to come up with a likely diagnosis.

Fortunately, this was the case with Nancy. An examination of her cervix revealed that it had been weakened, possibly by one or both of the D and Cs performed after her miscarriages. Although this probably wasn't a factor in the first miscarriage, it could have contributed to the second. And if untreated, it most certainly would interfere with a third pregnancy.

Nancy's complaints of abdominal pain led me to suspect that she also had fibroid tumors in her uterus that could cause the uterus to reject the fetus. To confirm this diagnosis, I ordered a hysterosalpingogram, or X ray of the uterus, which indeed revealed that I was right.

Armed with this knowledge, I was able to tell Nancy and Alan that with a proper pregnancy plan, I believed they had a good chance of having another child. However, I advised Nancy to have the fibroids surgically removed before attempting the next pregnancy. Indeed, a year and a half later, after a moderately difficult pregnancy, Nancy gave birth to a very healthy baby girl.

There are times, when despite our best efforts, the cause of the miscarriage remains a mystery. The patient history and exam may reveal nothing new. There is nothing in either the mother's or the father's history to suggest a reason as to why they lost a healthy child. Yet, as a physician, I cannot tell this couple that nothing went wrong, because if nothing had gone wrong, they would have had a baby instead of a miscarriage.

To these couples, I offer this advice: If you want a baby, don't be afraid to get pregnant. As I frequently say in this book, every pregnancy is different. There is a good chance that the problem that plagued your last pregnancy may lie dormant the next time. In addition, there are some steps you can take to increase your odds of success. Become an educated patient. Learn the early warning signs of possible problems. If you are aware of your body, perhaps a symptom that failed to set off a warning bell in the last pregnancy will not go unnoticed this time. Even if problems do occur, you may discover them early enough to do something about them.

Gathering the Clues

Why did it happen? Why did my neighbor come home with a healthy baby and why did mine die?

—Julie, two miscarriages, mother of a four-year-old son and a two-year-old daughter

---

CHECKLIST
The Post-Miscarriage Interview

1. Previous history of miscarriage, stillbirth, or premature labor.
2. Detailed account of current miscarriage. Discussion of symptoms, such as fever, bleeding, or unusual vaginal discharge, that could shed some light on the cause.
3. If relevant, possibility of chromosomal abnormalities on the part of parents or in family history (i.e., close relative with history of miscarriage or stillbirth).
4. Thorough gynecological history of the mother, including discussion of:

   · previous elective abortions
   · previous D and Cs (why were they performed)
   · history of infertility
   · any abnormal findings in pelvic exam
   · history of amenorrhea or menstrual loss
   · history of tubal or other surgery
   · history of infection
   · history or possibility of fibroids
   · possibility of DES exposure in utero

One of the cruelest things about miscarriage is that often nothing is learned from the tragic experience because the evidence that might have led to the discovery of the causes rapidly disappears. Unless prompt action is taken, valuable clues vanish and information that may be useful in preventing the next loss remains undiscovered.

In some ways, we must play the role of detective, trying to reconstruct what went wrong so we can learn from the experience, because history may repeat itself. In addition, in the process of gathering information, we may become aware of other related risk factors that we may have previously overlooked.

Time is of the essence. Within hours after the miscarriage, the tissue that was expelled will begin to deteriorate and become contaminated by outside bacteria. Symptoms of any maternal illness, such as hypertension or diabetes, that may have caused the miscarriage will also disappear as the moth-

5. A complete maternal medical history, including:

   - history of hypertension, diabetes, or other conditions that might affect pregnancy
   - family history of medical conditions that might affect pregnancy

6. Father's medical history whenever relevant

   - history of infection such as mycoplasma, chlamydia, or any other sexually transmitted disease

7. Physical exam of mother

   - check for uterine abnormalities
   - check for incompetent cervix
   - check for signs of DES exposure

8. Possible exposure to teratogens, that is, any agents such as radiation or drugs that can contribute to miscarriage.
9. Discuss any questions or feelings patient may have about the miscarriage.
10. Review of lifestyle. Any factors such as unusual stress, poor nutrition, smoking, or heavy alcohol consumption that may play a role in pregnancy loss.

er's body returns to its prepregnant state. Therefore, any tests or procedures on the fetus or pregnancy tissue, and in some cases on the mother, should be performed as soon as possible.

Here are some of the tests and procedures that may provide useful information.

1. *Karyotype of Fetal Tissue:* A chromosomal analysis of the fetal tissue or conceptus will reveal any chromosomal abnormalities that may have caused the loss. If a chromosomal problem is discovered, a genetic counselor can help the couple determine the likelihood of a miscarriage occurring again. Since this test is expensive, a doctor will not routinely order one unless a genetic problem is suspected, as in the case of a woman who has had several unexplained miscarriages or a family history that points to an inherited disorder. In some cases, a karyotype of the parents will also be performed.

2. *Cultures:* Fetal tissue can be cultured—that is, grown in a laboratory dish and analyzed—to determine if an infection such as chlamydia, mycoplasma, or Group B streptococcus (an organism found in the lower genital tract of about 40 percent of third-trimester women that could, in rare cases, cause complications) could have been responsible for the miscarriage. Once the problem is discovered, the mother can be treated and steps can be taken to prevent the organism from attacking future pregnancies.

3. *Photographs of Fetus:* A photograph taken while the facial features are still fresh could provide useful clues in combination with other test results. For example, a doctor may check for certain physical characteristics, such as an irregularly shaped head or forehead, that could indicate specific abnormalities or syndromes that may have caused the miscarriage.

4. *X rays of Fetus:* An X ray of the fetus will show any abnormalities of the bone tissue that may point to a possible cause.

5. *Tissue Studies:* Tissue samples may be sent to a pathology laboratory to be studied for any birth defects, chromosomal or otherwise, that may have contributed to the miscarriage.

6. *Examination of Mother:* If a maternal illness such as gestational diabetes is suspected, blood and urine must be collected from the mother immediately to be tested as evidence of the illness will quickly vanish with the end of the pregnancy.

7. *Ultrasound of Mother:* An ultrasound exam may be performed on the mother to detect any uterine abnormalities or growths in the uterus.

Even if the doctor is unable to pinpoint a single cause, the information that is gathered during this critical period may help a specialist, such as myself, better plan future pregnancies. In addition, the pieces of the puzzle may suddenly make sense when other symptoms begin to surface during a future pregnancy, and may help avert another tragedy.

Within six to eight weeks after the loss, the mother should undergo a complete physical examination to make sure she is healing properly. Based on the information gathered after the miscarriage, the doctor may decide to perform the following tests.

1. *Ultrasound:* An ultrasound exam may be performed to detect any uterine abnormalities, such as a misshaped uterus or fibroids. Unfortunately, the ultrasound may be inconclusive, and more invasive tests may be necessary.

2. *Hysterosalpingogram* (X ray of pelvic area): During this procedure, a special dye is pumped into the uterus through the vagina, followed by an X ray of the pelvic area. The dye helps clarify anatomical defects of the uterus and tubes, as well as any growths such as uterine fibroids. A hysterosalpingogram is usually performed on an outpatient basis at either a hospital or a special X-ray or diagnostic imaging facility.

3. *Hysteroscopy:* A hysteroscope is a tiny instrument that is used to open the cervix to allow the physician to look directly into the uterus. During this procedure, the physician should be able to locate any defects in the shape of the uterus, abnormal uterine growths, or scar tissue. In some cases, he will be able to remove these growths, sparing his patient the risk and trauma of major abdominal surgery. This procedure may be performed with a local anesthetic at the doctor's office.

4. *Cultures:* If an infection is suspected of having caused the miscarriage, cultures may be taken to make sure that the mother is free of the problem before attempting another pregnancy. A woman who is infection-prone may need to be monitored closely for infection throughout her subsequent pregnancies. In some cases, cultures will also be taken of the

culture of

father's sperm to make sure that he is free of any infections that could be passed back and forth.

As I've said earlier, all of this hard work may not yield a definitive answer. But more likely than not, you will be able to point to a specific problem and say with a degree of certainty, "Yes, this probably contributed to my miscarriage and we'll be ready for it next time."

However, even if you're able to pinpoint a specific problem, I want to remind you of something that I frequently tell my patients: Every pregnancy is different. The problem that caused one miscarriage may disappear the next time, and another one may surface. Never become overconfident that you have found The Answer.

To make my point, whenever I meet with a couple for the first time, I offer this analogy. Suppose your home had been burglarized by someone who gained entry through an open window. Well, you could simply close the window and assume that the burglar could not get in another way. But if you just did that, you probably wouldn't be able to sleep very well at night. More likely, you would not only close the window but lock every other window in the house, install an alarm system, buy a guard dog, and do everything else in your power to make sure that no burglar ever again gained access to your home.

This is how you must approach your next pregnancy. It is not enough to correct one or two problems and assume that everything will be fine. You must do everything in your power to anticipate problems before they happen and to protect your pregnancy against all possible threats. You must become a well-educated, "pregnancy literate" expectant mother who is well equipped to work closely with her doctor. In the end, you will be richly rewarded.

Choosing a Doctor: Breaking Up Is Hard to Do

My doctor was wonderful. I had gone to him since college and we'd been through a lot together. He held my hand during my two miscarriages. My husband and I cried on his shoulder. He's a terrific person and I will certainly go back and use him as a gynecologist after I finish having children. I know he was hurt when I decided to seek another opinion, but I felt that I had no other choice. He kept telling me everything was okay, but I didn't believe that having two miscarriages in a row was normal.

— Lisa, mother of nine-month-old girl

There are few relationships as intimate as the one between a woman and her obstetrician. A woman may reveal to her doctor secrets that she would keep from her best friend, or even her husband. Trust and confidence must be the foundation of this unique relationship. And yet, ironically, to get the best medical care possible, women must refrain from being too trusting. They must try to maintain some objectivity, and given the nature of this relationship, this is often most difficult to do.

We've all heard stories about doctors who are annoyingly patronizing, overly authoritarian, or sometimes downright surly to their patients. Most patients have very little trouble saying goodbye and good riddance to these kinds of doctors. I believe, however, that these extreme cases are few and far between. At the very least, most obstetricians are courteous to their patients and many of them make a genuine effort to be considerate and compassionate when patients are experiencing a crisis such as a miscarriage.

When it comes to medical care, however, nice is not enough. I have seen too many women cling to doctors who may have been wonderful at giving aid and comfort after a pregnancy loss, but who did far too little to prevent the loss from occurring in the first place. Often out of a misguided sense of loyalty, patients stick with doctors who may be model human beings but who, in my opinion, are not model physicians.

As I state repeatedly throughout this book, after a miscarriage it is not enough for a doctor to offer a few words of solace and then tell a patient to wait a few months and try again. To improve the chances of success for the next pregnancy, a doctor must be willing to undertake a thorough investigation of why the loss occurred. He or she must be willing to work closely with the patient to try to prevent it from happening again.

If you express your fears about having another miscarriage, many doctors will cooperate with your efforts to prevent a future loss. If your doctor is making a concerted effort to work with you, I feel you should give him a chance. Hopefully, both of you have learned from the past loss and are willing to put that knowledge to good use in a future pregnancy.

If, however, your doctor dismisses your concerns and doesn't seem interested in taking the time to properly guide you through the next pregnancy, I feel you should consider finding another doctor.

If you do decide to change doctors, you should not be burdened with feelings of guilt and disloyalty. Although we place a special emphasis on the doctor/patient relationship, never forget that the doctor is there to serve you, not vice versa. You are hiring a doctor to help you achieve a goal. That goal is having a baby. If you're not getting the results you need from your doctor, you owe it to yourself to find someone who can help you achieve that goal.

> My first child was born two months premature and suffered serious complications. During my second pregnancy, when I started spotting during the fifth month, I became very worried. I called my doctor and he said not to worry, this happens all the time. When I asked to see a specialist for a second opinion, he became very angry and said, "I'm the captain of this ship and I prefer that you don't see anyone else. There could be a misunderstanding, and if something goes wrong, I want to be in charge."
>
> — Diana, eight months pregnant

It's a good thing Diana had the sense to jump ship when she did. In spite of her doctor's objections, she came to see me for a consultation. By that time, she was already in serious danger of delivering even earlier than she had before and could have lost the baby.

I don't feel any doctor has the right to prevent a patient

from seeking a second opinion, especially one who has suffered as much as this patient. Medicine is not an exact science. Sometimes one doctor may see something that another may have overlooked. It happens to all of us, and rather than getting defensive, I feel there are times when a doctor should welcome another's input.

Not every doctor is capable of bringing a difficult pregnancy to a safe conclusion. I fear that some—albeit a minority—may allow a patient to miscarry before they will admit that they may not have the expertise to help her. In these cases, it is up to the patient to make her needs clearly known to the doctor, and if those needs are not met, she should have no qualms about switching in midstream.

The more assertive patients, those who exercise their right to change doctors, are often made to feel as if they are somehow at fault. Pam, one of my patients who sought a different doctor after each of three unexplained miscarriages, told me, "I have been accused of jumping from doctor to doctor, looking for a savior who could perform miracles instead of sticking with one who would help me solve my problem. But the fact of the matter is, not one of them ever attempted to deal with my miscarriages until after the fact."

Although it's easy enough to find a different doctor, finding a doctor with a different outlook may be a bit trickier. One of the best ways to learn about a doctor is through the recommendation of a contented patient, preferably someone who has been treated by that physician over a period of time and who knows what he is really like. Since a woman who has miscarried has special needs, I feel it is wise to get that recommendation from another woman who has experienced a pregnancy loss.

One source might be self-help or peer support groups that provide information and emotional support to people with similar problems. There are several groups around the country for women who have suffered infertility or pregnancy loss, including SHARE, RESOLVE, and, in my home state, New Jersey, MIDS. Valuable information is often exchanged at meetings, including the names of doctors with good track records.

Other valuable sources of information can be found at your

local hospital. For example, if the hospital has a social worker who counsels women who have miscarried, he or she may be able to refer you to a doctor who is particularly knowledgeable in this area. You can also check with the head of the Department of Obstetrics to see if she or he has a recommendation.

Once you gather a few names, see if you can meet with each doctor for a consultation. At the initial meeting, try to find out as much about him as possible. To do this effectively, you'll have to go beyond the standard questions (such as, "Do you allow husbands in the delivery room?") often asked by patients and home in on your specific problem. If you are worried about the possibility of another pregnancy ending in miscarriage, voice these concerns to each of the prospective doctors. Ask each of them directly what they will do to help prevent another pregnancy loss. While it's highly unlikely that any doctor will be able to devise a specific plan before he knows your complete history, he should be able to give you some idea of his overall approach. And if a doctor tells you up front that he doesn't believe miscarriage can or should be prevented, scratch his name off the list and keep on looking.

Before you select a doctor—not after you've signed on as a patient—is the time to bring up other pertinent subjects, such as the doctor's willingness to allow labor support other than a spouse into the delivery room, or his attitude toward patient education. If you've had a previous cesarean delivery and would like to try for a vaginal birth, be sure to ask if he shares the "once a cesarean always a cesarean" philosophy, or if he would be willing to try VBAC (vaginal birth after cesarean). If you want to be assured of greater access to your doctor, find out if he sets aside a special time for nonemergency calls when he will answer questions. Before you make your final choice, carefully assess which doctor you feel most comfortable with and will be able to forge the most effective partnership with.

If you do it correctly, the selection process can be time-consuming. If you consider, however, that it's probably one of the most important decisions you will ever make, the extra time it takes to find the right physician is well worth it. In the end, you will find the doctor who not only shares your philosophy on critical issues but who best suits your emotional and medical needs.

> I had to wait one to two hours before each appointment and when I finally got in to see my doctor, he was so rushed all the time that it hardly seemed worth it. He got annoyed when I asked questions. I'm over thirty-five and my first baby was very premature. I felt I needed someone who would give me close attention, who wasn't in it for the money.
>
> — Anita, seven months pregnant

I cringe whenever I hear patients complain about being kept waiting for appointments because I, too, am often guilty of running behind. The practice of obstetrics is an unpredictable one. We may try to schedule our appointments so that we can see patients promptly, only to have three women go into active labor in the same afternoon.

On the whole, however, patients should not be kept waiting by their doctors for inordinate amounts of time. Appointments should never be so tightly scheduled that every office visit automatically means an hour or two wait. If tardiness is a chronic problem in your doctor's office, you have the right to complain. It could just be that your appointments are always scheduled at a particularly busy period, such as lunchtime in a practice that services many working women. Perhaps by changing the times of your appointments, you could avoid the long waits.

When you do get in to see your doctor, you should never feel rushed or intimidated. No matter how busy he may be, you are entitled to a thorough examination at each prenatal visit, as well as enough time to ask whatever questions you may have. Your doctor should also use each visit as an opportunity to review important information such as how to check for labor contractions, how to recognize the warning signs of premature labor, and how to properly monitor fetal movements. It's up to you to make sure that you get everything you need to ensure a successful pregnancy.

You should never walk out of your doctor's office feeling

upset or angry. If you do, let your doctor know how you feel. In many cases, he may make a greater attempt to meet your needs. However, if you find that visits to your doctor are consistently frustrating and anxiety-provoking, it may be time to find another doctor.

Shopping for a Hospital

When you select an obstetrician, you're not only choosing the person who will assist in the delivery of your baby, you're also choosing the location and style of your delivery. Every practicing obstetrician is affiliated with one or more hospitals to which he can refer patients. In most cases, a doctor must have attending privileges within a certain medical facility or he cannot use the facility. But before I discuss how to choose a hospital, let me explain why I feel a hospital is the only safe place to deliver a baby.

As bad as many hospitals may be—and believe me, I sympathize with people who complain about the insensitivity and coldness of hospitals—the fact remains that giving birth anywhere else poses a significant risk to both mother and child. Although most births are perfectly normal, in the minority of cases where serious problems do arise, they need to be dealt with swiftly and effectively. Under the best of circumstances, labor is a stressful situation in which each contraction results in a reduction of oxygen to the baby. A perfectly healthy, normal baby can easily withstand the stress of labor. However, one that is developing problems may not. The early symptoms of fetal distress are often very subtle and can easily be overlooked. By the time the baby begins to show obvious signs of oxygen or circulatory deficiencies, he will require immediate medical attention. Every second counts. In the time it takes to get a mother from her home or birthing center to an appropriate medical facility, the baby—and, in some cases, even the mother—could lose their lives.

Women embarking on a pregnancy today rarely give any thought to the possibility of losing their lives while giving birth. Yet, as recently as fifty years ago, that wasn't the case.

Childbirth was a risky business. Consider this: In 1935, when many of your grandmothers were having children, over 12,500 maternal deaths due to childbirth or related complications were reported in the United States. Or, put another way, out of every 100,000 live births, about 582 mothers died. At that time, fewer than three out of five white—and presumably even fewer nonwhite—births took place in hospitals.

In large part due to the growing acceptance of hospital births, the use of antibiotics to combat infection, and better management of maternal illness, maternal mortality has dramatically declined. Today, with more than 99 percent of all deliveries performed in hospitals, the maternal mortality rate in the United States has dropped to about 300 per year, or about 9 per every 100,000 births. While it's tragic that in this day and age even one woman should lose her life in childbirth, within a relatively short period of time we have made tremendous strides in saving maternal lives.

We have also made tremendous strides in saving the lives of babies. In recent years, the rate of perinatal death, that is, the number of stillbirths and neonatal deaths, has also dramatically declined. In 1950, there were 29.8 infant deaths per every 1,000 live births in the United States, as compared to 10.5 in 1987. Although I feel that our rate of infant mortality is still too high and much can be done to reduce it, in a mere thirty years we have managed to cut it in half, a feat we could not have performed without the medical technology available in hospitals.

Critics of the medical establishment are quick to point out that the rise in hospital births and use—or abuse—of technology in the birthing process has precipitated the sharp increase in cesarean deliveries. They have a point. In 1965, a mere 4.5 percent of all babies were delivered by cesarean. By 1984, that number soared to 28.8 percent, and according to one recent study, if present trends continue, by the year 2000 it is likely that 40 percent of all babies will be delivered surgically.

Fear of the surgeon's knife and the impersonalized, high-tech approach to childbirth found in many hospitals have created a small but vocal group of childbirth activists who advocate delivery in a nonmedical setting, such as a birthing center or even the home.

I feel that this is an unfortunate trend, and that these critics are missing the point. Women should not have to choose between a technologically dominated hospital birth and the riskier—albeit more natural and humane—birth at home or in a birthing center. They should demand the right to have both the technological and humane, and I see no reason why they can't have both.

There are some positive trends emerging within the medical establishment in response to consumer unhappiness. Many hospitals are becoming less rigid and more flexible in their approach to childbirth. Educated consumers who are willing to shop around will in all likelihood be able to find a hospital that will accommodate their special needs.

Childbirth practices and procedures vary greatly from hospital to hospital. Some hospitals, especially those that are eager to attract consumers, are more responsive to patient needs and desires than others. However, beware of overzealous marketing practices that promise much and deliver little.

Throughout the country, many hospitals are offering specially designed birthing rooms that look more like hotel suites than hospital rooms for couples who want the emotional satisfaction of a home birth within the safety of a hospital. In addition, many hospitals are now luring customers by providing such amenities as special parent-education courses, childbirth preparation classes, sibling orientation programs, rooming-in facilities for parents who want to care for their babies at birth, and even twenty-four-hour helplines to assist nervous parents after they leave the hospital.

If you're lucky enough to live near several medical facilities, it's a good idea to visit as many of the labor and nursery facilities as possible and perhaps even sample some of the childbirth education classes before making your choice. While it's difficult to judge the quality of care without actually being a patient, it's possible to get a feeling for the overall atmosphere and attitude of the hospital personnel. Keep in mind that overcrowded, understaffed labor rooms do not bode well for a successful, nonsurgical delivery.

If you feel very strongly about delivering at one particular hospital, then you will have to select a doctor who is affiliated with that institution. The obstetrics and gynecology department can provide you with a list of names from which you can make your choice.

In addition to observing the facilities and general atmosphere, it's important to find out about hospital procedures. Here's a list of some of the questions you may want to ask your doctor or hospital representative.

1. Will my husband be allowed in the delivery room? (In most cases, the answer will be yes.)

2. Will I be allowed to bring in my own labor support, that is, a woman specially trained to assist couples during childbirth? (Although I recommend this for my patients, not all hospitals will allow you to bring more than one person to the labor room. See the subsection on labor support later in this chapter).

3. If your goal is a drug-free birth, find out if the hospital encourages natural or drug-free childbirth. Don't take their word for it; ask for actual statistics of drug-assisted versus non-drug births.

4. What is the hospital's rate of cesarean section compared to vaginal delivery?

5. If you've had a previous cesarean, will the hospital permit VBAC (vaginal birth after cesarean)? What are the statistics on VBAC—that is, how many procedures are attempted and what is the actual success rate? This figure reflects not only on the philosophy of the hospital but also on the competency of its staff.

6. What are the statistics on the number of breech births delivered vaginally? In many cases, an experienced, skillful obstetrical staff should be able to deliver breech presentations without resorting to surgery.

7. Are all maternity patients put on an electronic fetal monitor (EFM), or are they permitted to walk around?

8. Does the hospital have any mandatory "prepping" procedures, such as shaving the pubic area, that you may find objectionable?

As you and your partner formulate your own plan for delivery, other questions are bound to come up. Keep in mind that not all hospitals are as patient oriented as others. If you encounter a hospital administrator or staff member who is reluctant to answer your questions, it should give you some indication of the hospital's general attitude toward patients.

For most couples, the birth of a child is one of the most important moments of their lives. The right environment—one in which they feel safe, secure, and comfortable—can only enhance this momentous experience. Remember that you are paying for this service, and you should get the maximum result for your dollar.

Planning for Delivery

Other pregnancy books go into great detail about the stages of labor and delivery, so I won't repeat what you probably know already. What I will do, however, is arm you with the information you need to be an effective "partner" in labor and delivery. Here's some of the advice I give to my patients that I feel would be of benefit to all couples anticipating the birth of a child.

1. *Be familiar with your surroundings.*   Be sure to visit the labor and delivery floor of the hospital of your choice long before the onset of labor. When you arrive at the hospital in labor, both of you are bound to be a bit excited and disoriented. Knowing the location of vital places such as bathrooms, showers, telephones, and snack bars will help make you feel more at home and in control.

2. Work out a birthing plan ahead of time. When you first selected your obstetrician, you probably asked him a lot of questions about his views on patient participation, cesareans, EFMs, drug-free births, labor support, and whatever other topics were important to you. The fact that you chose him is an indication that you see eye to eye on the critical issues. Now's the time for all of you to work together to achieve your common goals.

Sometime during the last trimester, you, your partner, and your doctor should sit down and devise your strategy for labor and delivery. At this point, you three should discuss such issues as the use of EFMs, and whether or not you want to strive for a drug-free birth. Even if you're adamant about not wanting any medication to alleviate pain, I feel it's still important for the doctor to review your options just in case you change your mind. Many women find it comforting to know they have a few options from which to choose.

If you've had a normal pregnancy, and no complications are anticipated, you will probably require very little medical intervention during labor and delivery. Your doctor may want to use an EFM for short periods of time, but unless there is a problem, there is no reason to use a monitor throughout labor. In fact, in many cases, an EFM can actually hinder labor, because it prevents the patient from shifting positions, walking around, and performing other activities that can speed labor along. The overuse of EFM has also been cited as the major factor in the dramatic rise in cesarean deliveries. (For an in-depth discussion of EFM, see chapter 8.)

During this strategy session, it is also a good idea to stress your desire for a nonsurgical, vaginal delivery. Tell your doctor that you view surgery as a last resort and that you expect him to exhaust all other possibilities before he picks up the scalpel. Too often, cesareans are performed on the basis of the flimsiest of indications. For instance, unless an immediate, life-threatening situation is suspected, the fact that an EFM may detect a slowdown in fetal heart rate is not sufficient reason to rush to the operating room. Variations in fetal heart rate are often a normal reaction to labor. Other tests, such as a fetal blood sample or ultrasound, should be performed before the decision is made to deliver surgically. (See chapter 8, "Inside the Womb: Keeping Track of Your Baby from Conception to Birth," for more information on testing.)

Of course, in the case of a true emergency, a cesarean delivery can be a lifesaving procedure for both mother and baby. If it is performed unnecessarily, however, the mother is needlessly subjected to major abdominal surgery and both she and her infant are exposed to the serious complications that can develop from this procedure.

Bringing Your Own Labor Support

> Putting a husband in the delivery room and telling him to coach his wife in childbirth is like taking someone who has watched a few baseball games on television and then putting him on the playing field to coach the World Series.
>
> — Louise Rosenberg, certified childbirth educator and labor support person

Long before hospitals had delivery rooms, a woman in labor was traditionally cared for by midwives or other women who had previously given birth. By the second half of the twentieth century, however, most births took place in hospitals and women were denied the emotional support of being surrounded by family and friends during childbirth.

Within the past decade or so, in response to consumer demand, many hospitals have allowed husbands into labor and delivery rooms to coach their wives through the arduous task of childbirth. A half-dozen childbirth education classes were supposed to arm the couple with all they needed to know to get through this momentous occasion.

Although the presence of a loved one was a welcome addition to the labor room, many women still found that they missed being cared for by someone who knew exactly what they were going through, a woman who understood what labor contractions felt like and whose experience and advice could help them through the rough spots.

That's exactly the role that modern-day labor support per-

sons perform. Known as doulas, labor coaches, childbirth assist-
ants, or monitrices, these women not only provide support for
the mothers, they also help the fathers better guide their wives
through labor and delivery.

Typically, the labor support person meets with the couple
several times prior to delivery. At these meetings, she will
become familiar with the couple's views on such vital issues as
the use of medication for pain control and the role the husband
wishes to play during labor and delivery. (Some men want to
actively participate; others want to confine their responsibility
to providing a supportive presence.) During labor and delivery, the support person will try to help the couple achieve the
kind of delivery they had envisioned at their earlier meetings.

Unfortunately, not all hospitals allow a couple to provide
their own labor support and some doctors may feel threatened
by the idea. In my experience, however, I have found that a
good labor support person is a terrific asset to the birthing
process. She can help even the most nervous couples remain
calm and confident.

Studies support my point of view. A report in the *New
England Journal of Medicine* noted that women who were
attended to by other women during labor had shorter labors,
were more alert after delivery, and smiled and talked more to
their babies than those who lacked this support. From this
study, we can conclude that the woman who delivers with the
benefit of labor support has a better birth experience and,
consequently, is in a better frame of mind to assume the role
of mother.

Many of you have probably never even heard of labor support before and don't have the foggiest idea of where to find
this kind of help. If your doctor is enlightened on this subject,
he or she may be able to offer some referrals. If not, you can
probably get some referrals from your local chapter of the
Cesarean Prevention Movement, a leading advocate of labor
support. (See appendix.)

Being an educated "partner in pregnancy" can serve you
well in the delivery room. The better prepared you are for
labor, the better you and your partner will be able to stay calm
and in control of the situation.

Insurance: Read the Fine Print

My insurance coverage was inadequate, to say the least. It paid 80 percent of the cost of the physician up to $750—that didn't cover even a quarter of the bill—and it paid for hospitalization. But it didn't pay for any of the procedures that were necessary to prevent preterm birth, such as ultrasound, amniocentesis, or even for a simple nonstress test. It didn't cover the medication I took to control contractions and prevent premature birth. At the end of the pregnancy, my husband and I were $25,000 in debt and we took a second mortgage out on our house to pay the bills, but at least we had a beautiful, healthy baby. If the baby had been delivered prematurely, she might have died, and if she had lived, the medical bills would have been in the hundreds of thousands of dollars.

—Jackie, three miscarriages, mother of a three-year-old girl

When it comes to insurance coverage for maternity-related benefits, don't take anything for granted. Read your policy! You may be surprised to learn that your policy does not cover pregnancy-related expenses. Many policies do not.

Insurance coverage varies greatly from plan to plan; therefore, to be absolutely certain of what your benefits will be, you should carefully review your policy. If you're covered through a group plan at work, read your employee handbook or check with your company's personnel officer.

As a rule, many policies offer some kind of coverage for maternity-related expenses, including hospitalization, medical and surgical procedures done in and out of the hospital, and physician care. Some policies will cover a portion of prescription costs, although others will not. Since many of the medications used to prevent preterm labor can be very expensive, be sure to take this into account if you're shopping for a policy. If you're interested in working with a midwife, make sure your policy will cover her services, since many do not. Most policies will not cover routine office visits, or patient education programs, such as childbirth education classes.

While many policies will not pay for well-baby care, some

will pick up a portion of the tab if your baby needs special medical attention. Some policies, however, delay coverage of newborns for up to the first thirty days of life. This gap in coverage can be devastating if your baby requires expensive care in a neonatal nursery. Also, in many policies, you will need to switch to a family plan or a parent/child plan to ensure that your newborn will be covered.

The percentage of reimbursement as well as the deductible—that is, the portion of the bill that you're expected to pay out of pocket—also varies from plan to plan.

If you're planning on changing jobs or switching insurance companies—for example, if you decide to join your husband's plan—keep in mind that many policies require that you be enrolled for a certain period of time before the conception of a child in order to be eligible for maternity benefits.

You should also be aware that many plans have a ceiling on the total amount of reimbursement allowed in any one year for any member of the family. Although most of us never use up our coverage, remember that a premature infant in a neonatal nursery can run up a bill of several hundred thousand dollars before he is released from the hospital. To be on the safe side, make sure that your policy sets a realistic ceiling. If it doesn't, consider purchasing additional coverage for your family (make sure it covers newborns) through an excess major medical policy. These policies are usually fairly inexpensive and offer the kind of catastrophic coverage that many insurance policies do not.

In my experience, I have found that insurance companies are often penny-wise but pound-foolish. Many companies will balk at having to pay an extra dollar or two for preventive care—such as for the few extra prenatal visits needed by a woman at risk of premature birth—but will fork out hundreds of thousands of dollars to pay for one premie in an intensive care nursery. I have spent a good deal of my professional life trying to educate insurance companies to the folly of their ways. In many cases, I have been successful. For example, one of my high-risk expectant mothers was very upset because her insurance company refused to pay for the additional care she needed to prevent a premature birth. I wrote the company a detailed letter describing my prematurity prevention program, stressing how both the patient and the insurer benefit if a baby is carried to term instead of being delivered before he can live independently outside the womb. The company agreed that prevention was not only the best medicine, but was also sound economics. It agreed to pay for the extra care. The lesson to be learned from this is that when it comes to insurance coverage, don't take no for an answer. If your insurer does not cover prematurity prevention, it's up to you and your doctor to show the company how you both can benefit from this kind of coverage. Some companies are beginning to recognize the savings from prevention. I often write lengthy letters on behalf on patients, detailing the value of preventive care, and they often produce positive results. Ask your doctor to help you; if he is your advocate, he will.

Due to the rising cost of health care, many consumers are turning to health maintenance organizations (HMOs) that offer a wide range of services for one flat fee. Although some prepaid HMOs provide excellent care, I feel that these types of plans can work against consumers. In most cases, you must choose an obstetrician who is a member of the HMO. If you don't like any of the obstetricians enrolled in the plan, or if you feel that they lack the expertise to manage a high-risk pregnancy, you're out of luck. Unless you have other insurance coverage, you must either stay with the HMO or pay for another doctor out of your own pocket. If you are a member of an HMO, make sure that the group has at least one obstetrician with whom you feel comfortable. Also keep in mind that if your obstetrician leaves the HMO, you may be forced to switch to another doctor within the plan.

If neither your medical plan nor your husband's offers maternity coverage, don't neglect to purchase some on your own. As expensive as health insurance may be, in the end, it can prove to be a true bargain. Even a normal pregnancy can cost thousands of dollars in medical expenses. A problem pregnancy, or one that results in premature delivery, can cost tens or even hundreds of thousands. Therefore, it is critical that you do not embark on a pregnancy without proper insurance coverage for both you and your baby.

Work Leave

If you lived in France, you'd be entitled to two weeks' prenatal leave and up to twenty-six weeks of maternity leave at 90 percent of your pay. If you lived in Israel, you would receive on average twelve weeks' maternity leave at about 75 percent of earnings. If you lived in West Germany, you would receive nearly full pay for up to eighteen weeks after giving birth.

In fact, if you lived in any of 127 countries in the world, you would be guaranteed some kind of paid maternity leave.

Not so in the United States. Depending on who you work for and what state you live in, you may not be entitled to receive any maternity leave, paid or unpaid. This despite the fact that most doctors agree that it takes between six and eight weeks to recover from a normal pregnancy, and even longer to bounce back if the pregnancy runs into complications.

It's not just maternal welfare that is at stake. Child psychologists such as T. Berry Brazelton say that it is critical for the emotional development of infants to spend at least the first three months of life with their mothers.

Unfortunately, doctors and child psychologists don't write the laws. If we did, I doubt that we would sit idly by and tolerate a system in which more than half of all working women are not entitled to any maternity leave.

Working women who become mothers must recuperate on their own time by using up whatever sick or vacation days they have accrued. For many women, this means that when they return to work, they are unable to stay home if they get sick or to take a day off when they get exhausted.

In recent years, Congress has taken some steps to protect the rights of working women. In 1978, Congress passed the Pregnancy Discrimination Act, which mandated that employers who offer disability benefits must include pregnancy and maternity. Many employers, especially small companies, were unaffected by this law because they didn't offer any disability benefits in the first place. Most women have the misfortune of working for these kinds of employers.

A handful of states (including California, Hawaii, New Jersey, New York, Rhode Island) and the commonwealth of Puerto Rico have passed laws that require all employers to offer some kind of temporary disability insurance for almost all workers. As of this writing, thirty-three other states are considering similar legislation. Although this is a step in the right direction, the fact of the matter is that most women still have to fend for themselves.

Don't take your maternity leave for granted! Since maternity policy varies widely from company to company, check out your employer's plan to see exactly what you will receive. Don't despair if your employer doesn't offer any maternity leave, or if the leave is inadequate for your needs. Depending on the nature of your job and your relationship with your employer, you may be able to negotiate some time off on your own and/or part-time employment for a period of time after the birth of your child.

Don't forget that your doctor can be an important ally. If for any reason you must stop work earlier than expected, or require more time to recuperate than your company allows, he should work as an advocate on your behalf, making sure you get the time off you need and the benefits to which you are entitled.

There's a chance, albeit a slim one, that before you give birth, Congress may pass a law requiring some kind of unpaid maternity leave. For the past three years, Congress has been considering various proposals to mandate unpaid parental leave of up to eighteen weeks, at the very least, for men or women in cases involving birth, adoption, or a serious illness of a child. I strongly favor this type of "profamily" legislation and have written a letter of support to Colorado congresswoman Patricia Schroeder, who is one of the bill's cosponsors. I urge every couple who are even contemplating pregnancy—as well as those who are concerned about children—to take the time to sit down and write a letter to your congressmen and senators in support of the Family and Medical Leave Act.

As a doctor and a concerned human being, I believe that

no woman should have to go through a pregnancy with the added stress of knowing that after nine months she will be forced to choose between her baby and her job. In a world where most women work, and most mothers are in the workplace, we need to find a way to allow women to accommodate both roles.

FOUR

Partners in Pregnancy: Making It Work Together

Recently, in the course of a single afternoon, I had the opportunity to meet for the first time with two new patients who presented similar problems but starkly different patient styles.

The first, Sharon, a twenty-nine-year-old junior high school teacher, was accompanied by her husband, Bob. Over the past two years, they had suffered the emotionally wrenching experience of two late miscarriages. Since they both desperately wanted children of their own, they had decided to try one more pregnancy before abandoning their dream of becoming natural parents.

Sharon had come to me on the recommendation of a friend, a former patient of mine who, after five miscarriages, is now the mother of a three-year-old son. Sharon and Bob were hoping for a similar "miracle." Sharon said tearfully,

"Dr. Semchyshyn, I'm in your hands. Do whatever you think is best."

Later that afternoon, I met Laura, a thirty-four-year-old social worker who had delivered a premature baby two years earlier. Born at barely twenty-six weeks, the baby was blind as well as physically and mentally retarded. Laura and her husband, John, were contemplating having another child and they were naturally concerned about avoiding another premature delivery.

I explained to Laura that she had a 30 percent chance of experiencing premature labor again. She might deliver normally the next time, or she might go into labor even earlier. There was really no way to predict.

Before I could even discuss my prematurity prevention program, Laura opened up a massive briefcase and proceeded to show me more than a dozen articles on the subject of premature birth that she had clipped from various medical journals.

"Doctor, what do you think of this treatment?" she asked as we reviewed an article on the use of a new drug to inhibit labor contractions. Several hours passed as we discussed the pros and cons of various treatments, as well as my experiences with patients of my own.

At the end of our meeting, Laura promised that she would get back in touch as soon as she got pregnant. "I'm not going to be an easy patient," she warned. "I can't help feeling that my last doctor did too little, too late, and now my baby is paying for his mistakes. This time, I want to be very involved in my treatment."

I guess my story makes the kind of patient I prefer to treat self-evident. I don't worry about patients like Laura. I do feel uneasy, however, when I encounter well-meaning but overly passive patients like Sharon who say, "Doctor, I'm in your hands. You take charge." It's not that I'm shying away from the responsibility. If that was my goal in life, I would never have chosen the field of high-risk pregnancy. The uneasiness comes from the knowledge that I cannot be as effective with a passive patient as I can with one who, like Laura, is eager to share responsibility for her pregnancy.

You're the Twenty-four-Hour-a-Day
Caregiver

The reason that I prefer patients like Laura is that no matter how thorough and up-to-date a physician may be, he or she cannot take the place of an observant mother-to-be. We obstetricians may possess a wealth of medical knowledge, but when it comes to your body, you're the expert. Although your physician may carefully monitor your pregnancy by having you visit the office every few weeks or so, you're the twenty-four-hour-a-day caregiver of your pregnancy. If something starts to go wrong, you'll be the first to know—at least, if you've been educated to know what to look for. Therefore, I believe it is absolutely critical for patients to take an active role in their pregnancies, and for doctors to be willing to give their patients the tools they need to be effective "partners in pregnancy."

Doctors must learn to listen to their patients, and patients must learn how to talk to their doctors. Many patients who have come to me after suffering miscarriages or premature labor say that they tried to alert their doctors to various symptoms that didn't seem quite right, but their doctors often dismissed their complaints as unimportant. Susan, a thirty-two-year-old homemaker who had two miscarriages before I met her, is a case in point. Throughout her two unsuccessful pregnancies, Susan tried to tell her doctor that she thought something was terribly wrong. Unfortunately, the subtle sensations that she tried to describe did not set off any warning bells. "I was saying things like 'I feel a little achy,' and 'I feel a twinge here and a twinge there.' My doctor didn't think it sounded serious enough to see me and even though I was worried, I didn't push it," Susan recalled. Twice, she miscarried at about four months.

After Susan became my patient, she and her husband spent several hours in my office preparing for the new pregnancy. I carefully described the progression of a normal pregnancy and compared it to one that was headed for problems. To Susan, it was a revelation. The feelings and events she had experienced—dull backache, menstrual-type cramps, and a thicker-than-usual vaginal discharge—were classic warning signs of miscarriage.

"Had I known this before, I would have understood the urgency of the situation and insisted that my doctor see me. I didn't communicate well with him and he wasn't astute enough to pick up on what I was saying."

Susan's story has a happy ending. Once again, during the fourth month of her last pregnancy, she encountered the same problems as before. This time, however, at the first sign of backache and cramps, she came to my office for an examination. As a result, we were able to intervene in time to save her pregnancy. Last June, she gave birth to a 7-pound girl.

In a later chapter, I will explain Susan's physical problem—an incompetent cervix—and how we treated it. For now, the point I want to make is that like so many patients, Susan suffered from a condition I feel is the primary culprit in most miscarriages and premature labor—"pregnancy illiteracy." Susan didn't know how to describe what was wrong in terms that her doctor would understand. Nor did she herself understand the critical nature of her situation. The only cure is patient education, a prescription doctors and patients must fill together. If women learn to "read their bodies" and transmit this information to their doctors, I believe countless numbers of miscarriages could be averted.

In many cases, if we are alerted in time to a problem, we can do something about it. As I will explain later, during the past ten years we have seen the development of several effective treatments to stop premature labor and help mothers carry to term. Yet the rate of prematurity has not dropped. Ninety percent of the time we are helpless to stop the birth of infants who are born long before nature intended them to live outside the womb, because women come to us when it is too late for us to help. In most cases, women we *can* help have one thing in common. They sought treatment at the first sign of labor!

The moral is simple. Technology can only be effective if patients are educated. If patients are unaware of the signs of preterm labor and fail to seek help in time, all the technological breakthroughs of the past decade are rendered useless.

Sharing Information

In an ideal "pregnancy partnership," patients not only learn from doctors, but doctors learn from patients. Most doctors will agree that our learning should not stop the day we complete our formal education. In fact, we often learn far more from our practices than from any textbook. For instance, an articulate patient may describe a symptom in the sort of vivid language that could only come from someone who has experienced the sensation firsthand. Her description teaches us how to communicate better with other patients. The observations of a sensitive but open patient may help us break down the barriers surrounding a more reticent one who may be afraid to discuss her symptoms, fears, and anxieties.

The knowledge we gain from inquisitive, determined patients can be invaluable in many different ways. As you know, many of my patients come to me because they have specific medical problems that may complicate their pregnancies. For instance, I have a number of patients who are diabetic. They are at greater risk for premature labor and stillbirth, and may develop other problems. I also see a number of women whose mothers took DES, a drug that was used in the 1950s to prevent miscarriage. These women are also at special risk of miscarriage and premature labor. To their credit, I have found that many of these patients are often more knowledgeable about their specific problems than the average physician. Quite often, these women have linked up with groups like the American Diabetes Association or DES Action that provide support and up-to-the-minute information on research and treatments. These women have made it their business to thoroughly research their problems and to investigate options. Any doctor would be foolish not to listen to what they have to say and implement their suggestions if they are medically sound.

When a patient comes up with a good idea, it's a win-win situation. As well as helping the patient, it broadens the doctor's vision and contributes to his overall fund of knowledge. For example, a patient recently brought me a newspaper article touting the benefits of fish oil—from fatty fish like salmon and sardines—on the circulatory system. This was of particular interest to her because she had a circulatory problem that resulted in two stillbirths. Her sluggish circulatory system was unable to adequately transport enough blood to the placenta, and thus the fetus was starved of needed nutrients. Now that she was pregnant for the third time, this patient naturally wanted to do everything in her power to make this pregnancy a success. In addition to other therapies I had prescribed, she wanted to know if she should also be taking fish oil pills.

That evening, I reviewed some articles in medical journals on the benefits of fish oil and I decided that it could indeed be a helpful addition to her overall treatment. We'll never know for sure whether the fish oil made a difference, but today she is the mother of a four-year-old son. This experience confirmed what I had already believed: By sharing information with each other, doctors and patients can forge a strong alliance against the enemies of a successful pregnancy.

Some doctors may bristle at the notion that their patients may, on occasion, think of something that they did not. It may be hard for some doctors to accept the fact that they don't always have all the answers. Patients may have trouble accepting the fact that their doctors may not know everything there is to know. While I don't want to undermine people's confidence in their physicians, I do feel this attitude is counterproductive. In order to get the best medical care possible, patients must remember one thing—your doctor is human, not a computer. You cannot and should not expect your doctor to know the answer to every question on the spot. What you can and should expect is that if your doctor doesn't know the answer, he or she will not dismiss your question with a "Don't worry about it." The answer you are entitled to expect is this: "I don't know. Let's find out."

Where an idea comes from shouldn't matter. If it's good,

it should be respected. Many successful businesses have staked their fortunes on this philosophy. I recently read an article about the Maytag Company that said the company is so committed to getting employee input that it pays employees for any suggestions they make that are implemented. While this practice costs a lot of money, it appears, based on Maytag's product share and reputation, to be working. I think that medicine can learn some lessons from companies like Maytag. If we actively seek out input from our patients and are willing to implement a good idea, we will reap better results. In the case of pregnancy, that means healthier mothers and healthier babies.

Your Right to Know

I recently attended a medical conference where after I described my "partnership" with my patients and my emphasis on patient education, a colleague turned to me and said, "I'm afraid that if I told my pregnant patients to watch out for everything that could go wrong, I'd be scaring them half to death and, not only that, I'd be on the phone with them for the next nine months explaining away every ache and pain. Does the average patient really need to know about this in such detail?"

His question is a good one and it gets right to the heart of my partners-in-pregnancy program. My purpose is not to frighten mothers-to-be into a frenzy. Nor do I want my patients to spend every waking hour fixated on their pregnancies, ever watchful for signs of trouble. On the contrary, I encourage my patients to lead as active and normal a life as they possibly can. My goal is to educate patients so that they can differentiate between the normal signs of pregnancy and any abnormal developments that may threaten the health and well-being of their babies and themselves.

Through the years I have learned that an educated medical consumer makes the best patient. Women who truly understand the pregnancy process—who know the difference between a benign vaginal discharge and one that signals trouble, who can distinguish a labor contraction from a Braxton Hicks—rarely waste their doctor's time with unnecessary calls. The truth of the matter is that an educated patient can help a doctor save time and lives. At the first sign of real trouble, she will pick up the phone. She is "pregnancy literate"—she knows how to describe her symptoms in terms that are meaningful to her physician. Most importantly, she will alert her doctor to a problem while there is still time to do something about it. Very often, we are able to intervene before the minor headache becomes a major problem.

Patient education, however, is not just for the convenience of the physician. Patients are starved for it. It dismays me when women complain, as they often do, that they feel that their obstetricians are too busy to talk to them. Pregnant women— perhaps even more than other patients—have a strong need to feel knowledgeable and in control. Over the course of nine months, their bodies are undergoing a major metamorphosis. It is only natural for a woman to be concerned about labor and delivery and impending motherhood. Much of her anxiety stems from our natural fear of the unknown. When it comes to pregnancy, ignorance is not bliss. The more a patient knows about pregnancy and the workings of her body, the more relaxed and secure she will feel. Since I believe that stress plays a major role in the outcome of a pregnancy, the prognosis for this educated patient is better than for one who is kept in the dark.

There are some people—doctors and patients alike—who may dismiss this kind of patient education as unnecessary. They may ask, Since most pregnancies are uneventful, do we really need to educate all women to the warning signs of trouble? The answer is yes. We can't always pinpoint which pregnancies will make it to the home stretch without a hitch and which will hit a snag. While there are some women who may be at higher risk of miscarriage and premature labor than others, the fact of the matter is, these occurrences can happen to anyone. Therefore, I feel it is critical that all pregnant women are at least familiar with the next chapter, "How to Monitor Your Pregnancy."

The goal of patient education is to prevent problems from happening in the first place. As the saying goes, knowledge is power. This is especially true when it comes to pregnancy. In many cases, the educated patient has the power to stop a threatened miscarriage, or to spare her child from the risk of premature birth. I believe it is the right of every patient to have this knowledge, and it is her obligation to put it to good use.

FIVE

How to Monitor Your Pregnancy

My doctor told me to call him if anything unusual happened. But when you're pregnant for the first time, everything seems unsual.

— Terry, mother of a two-year-old girl, reflecting on her past pregnancy

During pregnancy, many women feel like strangers in their own bodies. Something new is happening almost every day and often it's difficult to distinguish between the usual and the unusual.

The following checklist will help you differentiate between the normal bodily changes that should occur during pregnancy, and those that are symptoms of potential problems. It will also help you identify and track abnormalities as soon as they occur, so you can alert your doctor at the earliest sign of trouble.

Keep in mind that just because you may have one or two abnormal symptoms does not mean that your pregnancy is headed for trouble. However, these symptoms could be warning signs and a call to your doctor is warranted.

For some of you, this checklist will be easier to follow than for others. For example, if you are already aware of the bodily changes that occur each month during the menstrual cycle, and are sensitive enough to your body to know when you're getting sick before a slight cold blossoms into a sore throat and fever, you're ahead of the game. However, if you've never felt a menstrual cramp in your life, and could walk around for two days with the flu before knowing it, you're going to have to be extremely conscientious about learning how to stop and listen to your body.

First Trimester

What's Normal and Why It's Happening

AMENORRHEA (MENSTRUATION STOPS)

The menstrual cycle lasts about 28 days and is divided into two phases. In the first half, or estrogen phase, the ovary prepares to release an egg or ovum. At the same time, the uterus is preparing for pregnancy. As cells within the uterine wall, or endometrium, rapidly multiply, the wall grows thicker. In the second half of the cycle, or the progesterone phase, the ovary releases the egg. If pregnancy does not occur, the egg is absorbed by the body and the uterine lining is expelled through the vagina during menstruation. If pregnancy occurs, the fertilized ovum is safely lodged in the uterine wall and nourished by the rich lining.

MILD SWELLING

About 75 percent of all pregnant women experience some mild swelling, often around the ankles. It's nothing to worry about unless you notice a sudden increase in swelling or tenderness, as you will see later on in this section.

INCREASED SALIVATION

No one knows why this happens, but some women experience a dramatic increase in saliva. It's harmless, but can be very annoying if the increase is significant.

CHANGES IN BREASTS

During pregnancy, your body produces increased amounts of the hormones estrogen and progesterone. The increased levels of these hormones are responsible for many of the physical and emotional changes women experience during pregnancy. Swelling of the breasts and increased pigmentation in already darkened areas, such as nipples, are just two of these changes.

INCREASED URINATION

If it seems like you're spending your entire first trimester in the ladies' room, don't worry about it as long as the urine looks normal and there's no pain or burning upon urination. Increased urination very early in pregnancy is probably caused by hormonal changes. As the pregnancy progresses, the expanding uterus may press on the bladder, stimulating urination. Although this can be very annoying, it's also perfectly normal.

SLIGHT INCREASE IN VAGINAL DISCHARGE

Due to hormonal changes, you may experience a slightly thicker than usual discharge. Become familiar with what your normal pregnancy discharge looks like, because as you will see further on, any variation from the norm could indicate an infection or other problem. This discharge should not have a foul or unpleasant odor. If it does, check with your doctor.

HEARTBURN, INDIGESTION, CONSTIPATION

During pregnancy, hormonal changes relax or slow down your digestive system. Although this can cause minor discomfort, it's for a good cause. The slower transit time gives the body more time to absorb nutrients from the food, which in turn support the new life growing inside of you. Eating several smaller meals a day may help alleviate some of these annoying symptoms. The magnesium supplement I recommend for all my patients—500 milligrams of magnesium gluconate taken four times a day—should also help relieve the indigestion.

SORE, BLEEDING GUMS

Due to increased blood supply, the gums swell and can become highly sensitive. It is imperative that every pregnant woman see her dentist early in her pregnancy to ensure that the damage to her gums is minimized. I advise my patients to take 500 milligrams of vitamin C, which helps reduce gum inflammation and strengthen the gum tissue. Some women have found relief by switching to a toothpaste for sensitive teeth and gums.

MORNING SICKNESS (NAUSEA AND VOMITING)

About half of all pregnant women experience some form of "morning sickness," which is characterized by feelings of queasiness and nausea and occasional vomiting, and is caused by hormonal changes. Although many women experience these feelings upon waking, they can also be triggered by exposure to certain foods and odors. Extreme fatigue, fasting for too long a period, or binge eating can also bring on the problem. By the way, morning sickness can strike at any hour of the day or night. Excessive nausea and vomiting are not normal, as you will see later. Antacids are helpful if taken as frequently as every two or three hours, and pose no risk to either mother or baby.

SKIN CHANGES

Due to changes in pigmentation brought on by hormonal shifts, what's dark gets darker. Some women develop a dark line straight down their abdomen. Nipples also get noticeably darker. The dramatic increase in blood volume may cause other changes. Some women may notice tiny veins called spider nevi appearing on the upper part of the body, including the hands and face. Although they may pose a cosmetic annoyance, these changes are harmless and disappear after pregnancy.

OCCASIONAL DIZZINESS, FEELING FAINT

During pregnancy, blood pressure often drops below normal levels. If this happens, it can result in feelings of dizziness or lightheadedness. A quick check with the blood pressure cuff will probably reveal the drop in pressure. When this happens, the best thing to do is to lie down on your side and rest. (Lying on your back will make your blood pressure drop even further, because in that position the uterus presses against the blood vessels delivering blood to and from the heart, and so can hamper circulation.) Sudden fainting is a more serious sign, as we will see later.

FATIGUE, INSOMNIA

You're exhausted but you may not be able to sleep. There are a lot of changes going on in your body and it may take a while for your system to get used to them. I hate to keep blaming everything on hormones, but the change in estrogen and progesterone levels may be contributing to your sleeplessness. To compensate for loss of sleep, rest whenever you can. Avoid taking any medication to help you sleep. Some patients find a cup of warm milk before bedtime helpful. Don't despair, though; things will get better. A lot of my patients tell me they make up for the loss of sleep during the second trimester.

MOOD CHANGES, ANXIETY, FEAR

Those hormones are at it again. One minute you can be feeling euphoric and the next down in the dumps. However, hormones alone are not responsible for these mood swings. Your own fears and ambivalent feelings also play a major role. On the one hand, you may be thrilled about the pregnancy and on the other, concerned about the impact the new life will have on your life. If you've experienced a previous loss or losses, you're probably even more anxious about the outcome of this pregnancy. Whatever your past experiences may be, the first three months can be a tense time for all women. This is a time when emotional support from family and friends is as critical as excellent medical care.

What's Not Normal and What It May Mean

BACKACHE (A NAGGING LOWER-BACK ACHE OR
PAIN)

It may just be back strain: Did you carry a heavy package
or perform any unusually strenuous activity that may have
resulted in a sore back? However, it could also be a symptom
of a more serious problem, such as a backward-tilted uterus,
that could result in a miscarriage. If it persists for more than
a day, call your doctor. If the back pain is accompanied by
other symptoms on this list, don't wait, call your doctor immediately. NO MATTER WHAT PEOPLE MAY TELL YOU, IT IS NOT
NORMAL TO HAVE CHRONIC BACK PAIN THROUGHOUT PREG-
NANCY.

SUDDEN SWELLING OF LEGS, HANDS, OR FEET,
PUFFINESS IN THE EYES

You wake up one morning and notice that your shoes are
suddenly a size too small, your socks leave an imprint on your
calves, and your wedding ring doesn't fit. The sudden onset of
swelling could be a symptom of any number of potentially
serious conditions, such as hypertension or edema (fluid retention). Do not self-medicate with diuretics, but call your doctor
immediately. A day of bed rest with your feet elevated may do
the trick, or your doctor may prescribe other treatments, depending on the cause of the swelling.

GAIN OF MORE THAN 2 POUNDS PER WEEK

Rapid weight gain could be a sign that you're overeat-
ing. Before it gets out of hand, call your doctor or consult a
registered dietician for some nutrition counseling. However, sudden weight gain can also be a symptom of a more
serious problem, such as excess fluid retention (see the pre-
ceding section on swelling) or diabetes. It could also be a
sign that you are carrying more than one baby, something to
consider if you've been on fertility drugs or if twins run
in your family. DON'T SELF-DIAGNOSE. REPORT ANY
WEIGHT GAIN OF MORE THAN 2 POUNDS PER WEEK TO YOUR
DOCTOR.

FREQUENT FAINTNESS, FEELINGS OF DIZZINESS,
HEADACHES, BLURRED VISION

In the movies, pregnant women may faint at the slightest provocation, but not in real life. Although it may be normal to occasionally feel faint or dizzy during the early stages of pregnancy, it is definitely not normal to faint or constantly feel dizzy or woozy. Nor is it normal to suffer from constant, painful headaches or blurred vision. Any of these symptoms could indicate a more serious underlying problem, such as a sudden drop or increase in blood pressure, an ectopic pregnancy, a ruptured ovarian cyst, or even a kidney infection. CALL YOUR DOCTOR IMMEDIATELY. YOU SHOULD BE EXAMINED AS SOON AS POSSIBLE.

CONTINUOUS OR INTERMITTENT ABDOMINAL
PAIN

Abdominal pain could be caused by an ectopic pregnancy, fibroid tumors, or even a nonpregnancy-related problem, such as appendicitis. Don't take antacids and wait to see what happens. Call your doctor. He will probably ask you about other symptoms, such as fever, bleeding, dizziness, or anything else that may shed some light on the problem.

MENSTRUAL-TYPE CRAMPS

Menstrual cramps are caused by uterine contractions. Despite what other pregnancy books may say, it is not normal to experience these types of cramps during pregnancy. In fact, it is often an early warning sign of an impending miscarriage, or of a problem such as progesterone insufficiency, or even a tilted uterus. The symptom by itself provides us with little information, but combined with other symptoms—spotting or bleeding, backache, unusual vaginal discharge—could be meaningful and should be reported to your doctor.

BURNING SENSATION ON URINATION, CLOUDY
URINE, OR BLOOD IN URINE

Pregnant women are more prone to urinary tract infections, and women who normally have these infections are at even greater risk. In fact, about 10 percent of all expectant mothers will suffer from cystitis, an infection of the bladder, located in the lower urinary tract. The symptoms are burning or discomfort upon urination, any blood in the urine, or an unusual color to the urine. Cystitis can be easily managed by antibiotics. If untreated, however, the infection can spread to the upper urinary tract, including the kidneys, and could result in pyelonephritis, a potentially life-threatening condition for both mother and baby. Untreated urinary tract infections are a major culprit in premature labor, low-birth-weight infants, and stillbirth. To avoid infection, drink eight glasses of water a day and observe good bathroom hygiene (that is, wipe from front to back so bacteria from the rectum do not enter the vagina.) IF YOU SUSPECT YOU HAVE AN INFECTION, CALL YOUR DOCTOR IMMEDIATELY FOR AN APPOINTMENT. Blood in the urine could also be a sign of other problems, as you will see later on.

SEVERE NAUSEA OR VOMITING

Many pregnant women occasionally feel queasy and nauseous and may even vomit (see the earlier entry on morning sickness). Excessive nausea and vomiting are not normal. They can be signs of a more severe problem, such as a kidney infection, flu, a molar pregnancy—a rare condition in which the placenta forms cysts and cannot support an embryo—or even food poisoning. Excessive nausea and vomiting can lead to a problem, because a woman who suffers from these symptoms is probably not eating enough to provide the baby and herself with adequate nutrition. In severe cases, medication may be prescribed and hospitalization may even be required. IF YOU FEEL SICK AND NAUSEOUS FOR MORE THAN A DAY, CALL YOUR DOCTOR.

RASH OF UNKNOWN ORIGIN

A strange rash could indicate a simple allergic reaction to something you ate, or it could be a sign of a more menacing illness, such as German measles, chicken pox, or even Lyme disease, a potentially lethal disorder that is spread by the deer tick and can cause serious harm to the fetus. Don't take any chances; if you have a rash, call your doctor.

CHILLS, FEVER, OR SHAKES

Chills, fever, or shakes could be signs of anything from a viral infection to a kidney infection to an ectopic pregnancy. It could also be a sign of an infection of the amniotic fluid that is surrounding the baby. Whatever the cause, your doctor needs to know about it. IT IS ESPECIALLY CRITICAL THAT YOU DO NOT LET A FEVER OVER 101 DEGREES GO UNATTENDED, SINCE IT CAN JEOPARDIZE YOUR PREGNANCY.

UNUSUAL VAGINAL DISCHARGE

Although it's normal to have a somewhat thicker discharge during pregnancy, this discharge should not be so thick that it is noticeably different. It should definitely not be mucousy. A mucous discharge—similar in texture to egg white—could be a sign of an incompetent or weakened cervix that is opening, allowing the cervical mucus to seep through. A thick, foul-smelling discharge could indicate the onset of a vaginal infection, especially if it is accompanied by a burning or itching sensation. Infection can result in miscarriage or premature labor, and should be treated as soon as possible. A change in vaginal discharge is an important symptom that must be reported to your doctor immediately. He will need to examine you to determine the cause of the discharge, and the possible treatment.

CHRONIC EXHAUSTION, DEPRESSION

Some fatigue is normal in pregnancy, especially in the first trimester when your body and you are adjusting to a lot of new changes. Constantly feeling exhausted to the point where you can barely drag yourself out of bed, or chronic feelings of depression and tiredness are not normal. In fact, these symptoms may be a sign of anemia or another nutritional deficiency. Don't suffer in silence. Call your doctor for help.

GUSH OF FLUID FROM VAGINA

A watery trickle or gush of fluid from the vagina could indicate a leak of the amniotic fluid or the premature rupture of the membranes protecting the fetus. ANY RELEASE OF

FLUID FROM THE VAGINA COULD BE VERY SERIOUS AND YOU MUST NOTIFY YOUR DOCTOR IMMEDIATELY.

DIARRHEA, CONSTANT URGE TO MOVE BOWELS

Diarrhea could be the result of food poisoning or a viral infection, especially if it's accompanied by achiness and fever. Obviously, if you have diarrhea, let your doctor know about it. HOWEVER, IF YOU FEEL THE CONSTANT URGE TO MOVE YOUR BOWELS BUT DON'T, IT COULD INDICATE A PROBLEM WITH A TILTED UTERUS. The uterus could be pressing on the bowel, causing the constant urge to defecate. If not properly managed, a tilted uterus could result in a miscarriage. BE VERY SPECIFIC IN DESCRIBING THIS SYMPTOM TO YOUR DOCTOR. If you are not clear in your description, it could very easily be mistaken for cramps or indigestion.

BLEEDING, SPOTTING

YOU MUST NOTIFY YOUR DOCTOR IMMEDIATELY OF ANY SIGNS OF VAGINAL SPOTTING OR BLEEDING. I strongly disagree with other books that say that spotting and bleeding during pregnancy are "normal" for some women. Although some women who have experienced these symptoms may go on and carry to term, many will not. Therefore, it is important that each case of spotting or bleeding be carefully evaluated. The first thing that must be considered is, what is the cause? At this stage of the pregnancy, bleeding accompanied by pain could indicate an ectopic pregnancy, a life-threatening condition that must be treated as soon as possible. Bleeding could also be a sign of an impending miscarriage, or of a vaginal or urinary tract infection, among other possibilities. Both spotting and bleeding could indicate a progesterone deficiency, especially if the expectant mother also complains of menstrual-type cramps and backache. However, slight spotting or bleeding could also be caused by something as simple as an irritated hemorrhoid. When it comes to bleeding or spotting, don't play guessing games. You and your doctor should carefully consider all the possibilities based on your past history and current symptoms.

**What's Happening to Your Baby: The Critical
First Trimester**

The miracle of life begins with one single cell. About 266 days—or 200 million cells later—a baby is ready to be born. At the same time as the mother's body is outwardly changing to accommodate the new life, there are a great many exciting changes occurring inside her womb.

PERIOD OF THE OVUM: FIRST WEEK OF
DEVELOPMENT

Conception is a process that begins with the uniting of the woman's egg and the man's sperm. The egg is fertilized in the fallopian tube. At the moment of fertilization, the sex and genetic makeup of the baby are determined.

As I discussed in greater detail in chapter 2, every body cell contains a nucleus. Inside the nucleus, there are 46 chromosomes, or 23 pairs, with the exception of the nuclei of the sperm and egg. These special cells only have 23 chromosomes, and for good reason. When these cells unite, they each contribute their 23 chromosomes to the newly formed life, creating a new cell with the normal 46 chromosomes.

The fertilized egg or ovum, now complete with its 23 pairs of chromosomes donated by each parent, begins to divide as it journeys through the fallopian tube to the uterus, or womb. This cluster of cells, called a blastocyst, floats freely throughout the uterine cavity. About ten days after fertilization, it attaches to the lining of the uterus in a process called nidation. The process of conception ends when the blastocyst is safely ensconced in the uterine lining.

Although exact statistics are not available, anywhere up to 75 percent of all pregnancies may be lost before the blastocyst attaches to the uterine lining. In most cases, the woman never even knows she has become pregnant, since she has not experienced period loss. When a pregnancy ends before it can be diagnosed, it is called a chemical pregnancy.

PERIOD OF THE EMBRYO: THE SECOND TO THE
EIGHTH WEEK OF DEVELOPMENT

The mass of cells begins to differentiate, forming the embryo, the placenta, the umbilical cord, and the amniotic sac. The placenta, which develops on the inner wall of the uterus, transports oxygen and nutrients to the embryo and excretes its waste product through the umbilical cord. The baby floats in a watery cushion, protected against outside pressure or accidental blows.

Organ development proceeds at a spectacular pace as the brain and heart begin to form. The embryo begins to look more human as limbs begin to grow and facial features become more apparent.

At the end of the second month, the embryo has become a fetus.

PERIOD OF THE FETUS: NINTH WEEK TO
DELIVERY

The third month marks the formation of the external genitals and the beginning of the development of the reproductive organs. The baby can now move around in the amniotic sac, but the mother will not feel any movement until the middle of the next trimester.

By the end of the first trimester—or the first three months of life—the baby weighs about 1 ounce and is about 3 inches long.

Second Trimester

What's Normal and Why It's Happening

STUFFY NOSE, SINUS PROBLEMS

Due to hormonal changes, mucous membranes inside the nostrils swell, causing congestion.

MUSCLE CRAMPS OR SPASMS

Some cramping is caused by the slowing down of the circulatory system. Although these cramps may be painful, they're harmless. Cramping in the upper thigh may be caused by a spasm of one of the two round ligaments in the front of the uterus; it is usually triggered by a change in position (for example, a twisting motion done inadvertently when going from sitting to standing). A sharp, shooting pain emanates from the side of the uterus down to the groin. To ease the spasm, try to relax and lean toward the pain. If you tense up and pull your body weight away from the side that hurts, which you may do instinctively, you run the risk of irritating the uterus further. The uterus may contract, causing even more pain.

QUICKENING, OR FETAL MOVEMENTS

Toward the end of the second trimester—by the twentieth week for new mothers and the eighteenth week for those who already have children—most women begin to feel some fetal movements. Although the sensation may vary from woman to woman, those early feelings are often described as a "butterfly moving inside" or a slight "fluttering sensation."

MILD SWELLING

Due to the increased blood volume, many women experience mild swelling in legs, hands, and feet.

CONSTIPATION

The slowdown of the digestive system caused by hormonal changes can cause constipation. Although it may be uncomfortable, it is not dangerous and is best treated through dietary changes. (See "Good Nutrition: Building a Firm Foundation" in chapter 6.)

NAUSEA DISAPPEARS, APPETITE INCREASES

You've finally gotten your "sea legs" and are now getting acclimated to the changes in your body brought about by the pregnancy. You're eating more because you're hungrier, and that's the way nature intended it. From now until delivery, you should gain on average about 1 to 1½ pounds per week to provide you and your baby with optimum nutrition.

SLIGHT INCREASE IN VAGINAL SECRETIONS

From the beginning of pregnancy you've probably noticed that your vaginal secretions are thicker than usual. This is perfectly normal and, once again, is a result of hormonal changes. Although the secretions are slightly thicker, they should not be accompanied by excessive itching or have an unusual odor.

FEELING ENERGETIC

By now the fatigue of the first trimester should be a bad memory. You're probably happier, more energetic, and more in control.

ANXIETY, ESPECIALLY FOR HIGH-RISK PATIENTS OR WOMEN WHO HAVE EXPERIENCED PREVIOUS LOSSES

As well as things may be going, you still may have a nagging fear that something will go wrong. These fears are natural, and you may experience them until delivery day. Unless these feelings are accompanied by specific symptoms, or a strong belief that something is definitely going wrong, I advise patients not to be overly concerned. Don't bottle up your emotions. Talking about your fears with your doctor, midwife, labor support person, spouse, or another pregnant woman in a similar situation can be useful. (See chapter 10, "With a Little Help from Your Friends.")

BREASTS LESS TENDER

More good news. Although your breast size may have increased dramatically, your breasts are no longer sore and tender.

VARICOSE VEINS

In pregnancy, you learn to take the bad with the good. An expectant mother's blood supply increases by nearly 45 percent to meet the needs of both herself and her baby. This places a greater demand on the veins, which can become swollen and bulge through the skin.

HEMORRHOIDS

Hemorrhoids, a type of varicose vein in the rectum, can be caused by constipation and the pressure exerted by the growing uterus. They can be very unpleasant, often causing itching and burning, and may sometimes bleed. Warm baths help, but if the pain becomes too annoying, your doctor may prescribe a cream or ointment.

What's Not Normal and What It May Mean

SUDDEN SWELLING

In the first trimester we worried about sudden swelling because it might be a symptom of excessive fluid retention or hypertension. Now we have a new worry: preeclampsia, which affects about 5 to 7 percent of all pregnancies and doesn't usually strike until the second half of pregnancy. Preeclampsia is characterized by edema, hypertension, and kidney malfunction. If caught in its earliest stages, it can usually be treated successfully. If it is allowed to continue, it could develop into a far more serious condition, eclampsia. If you notice any kind of unusual swelling—suddenly your shoes feel tight or you can't get into a pair of gloves—call your doctor.

LESS THAN AVERAGE WEIGHT GAIN, UNDER ONE POUND PER WEEK

If you're not gaining weight steadily, it could be a sign that you're not eating enough, and you need to talk to your doctor or nutritionist about improving your diet. It could also mean, however, that your pregnancy is in distress, or that the fetus is not developing properly and may have a condition known as intrauterine growth retardation or IUGR, which means that the baby is small for his gestational age. IUGR could be caused by a malfunctioning placenta or by maternal illness. If you notice that your weight gain is inadequate, or that you're suddenly losing weight, notify your doctor.

NO FETAL MOVEMENT BY TWENTIETH WEEK, SUDDEN CHANGE IN FETAL MOVEMENT

The lack of movement could mean that your baby is exceptionally quiet or, in the case of a first-time mother, you may not know what you're actually feeling. It could also be a sign that something is going wrong. Your best bet is to check with your doctor so that he or she can perform the appropriate tests.

After about six months, fetal movement becomes more frequent. Some babies may be extremely active, although others may be more sedentary. For further explanation, read, in chapter 6, "Your Home-Care Program," on how to monitor fetal activity.

BRAXTON HICKS CONTRACTIONS, OR STIFFENING
AND HARDENING OF THE ABDOMEN

At about the same time you begin to feel fetal movement, you may also become aware of an occasional uterine contraction (and I do mean occasional). During these times, you may feel a stiffening and hardening of the uterus. Within a few seconds it should return to its soft, normal state. These are known as Braxton Hicks contractions. One or two contractions in the course of a day is no cause for alarm. However, if you notice a sudden increase in uterine activity, or have more than four contractions in an hour, you should call your doctor. (Look in chapter 6, "Your Home-Care Program," for more information on how to monitor for contractions.) IT IS NOT NORMAL TO HAVE FREQUENT AND REGULAR CONTRACTIONS BEFORE YOUR DUE DATE, AND IT COULD BE A SIGN OF PRETERM LABOR.

BLEEDING OR SPOTTING

As discussed in the first-trimester section of this chapter, bleeding can indicate a number of problems, some major, some minor. That's why it's important to call your doctor at the first sign of blood. In the second half of pregnancy, vaginal bleeding could be a sign of two potentially serious problems for mother and baby: placenta previa and abrupto placentae. In placenta previa, the placenta partially or completely covers the cervix. Unless treated immediately, this condition can lead to miscarriage or premature labor, and the mother is at risk of internal hemorrhaging. In cases of abrupto placentae, the placenta becomes detached from the uterine wall. If the separation is severe, the fetus can be deprived of oxygen and nutrients, which can be extremely dangerous. Abrupto placentae can occur prior to or during labor. Another symptom of abrupto placentae is abdominal pain or a sudden drop in blood pressure. (For more information on placental problems, read chapter 1, "The Causes of Miscarriage and Premature Birth.") Bleeding or spotting could also be a sign of a vaginal or kidney infection. If you're spotting or bleeding, be sure to check for contractions and other symptoms of preterm labor, including menstrual-type cramps, pelvic pressure, diarrhea, and unusual vaginal discharge. REMEMBER, CALL YOUR DOCTOR IMMEDIATELY AT THE FIRST SIGN OF BLOOD.

ABDOMINAL PAIN

Any kind of abdominal pain should immediately be reported to your doctor. It could be a symptom of any number of problems, including fibroid tumors, abrupto placentae, appendicitis, or even a case of the flu.

GUSH OF FLUID, TRICKLE OF FLUID FROM VAGINA

You could be leaking amniotic fluid. Or perhaps your baby moved in such a way that he exerted pressure on your bladder, causing a quick release of urine. If the fluid has a strong, sharp odor like that of ammonia, it is probably urine and you can breathe a sign of relief. However, if the discharge smells slightly fishy, it could be amniotic fluid. Regardless of what you think caused the loss of fluid, call your doctor immediately for further instructions.

UNUSUAL VAGINAL DISCHARGE

By this time, you know what a normal discharge in pregnancy looks and smells like. If there is any change, either in consistency or odor, call your doctor. A thicker-than-usual discharge accompanied by itching could be a sign of infection. A mucous discharge, often the consistency of egg white, could indicate an incompetent cervix.

MENSTRUAL-TYPE CRAMPS

As we discussed in the first-trimester section of this chapter, the achy, crampy feeling that many women experience during menstruation is also a sign of uterine contractions that could result in miscarriage or premature labor.

PELVIC PRESSURE, PAIN IN LOWER ABDOMEN, BACK, OR THIGHS

Any unusual pressure felt in the pelvic area or lower abdomen, back, or thighs should be reported to your doctor. Many women describe this sensation as feeling "as if the baby is trying to get out" or as if they are "sitting on the baby's head." What these women are actually feeling are uterine contractions that could be a sign of preterm labor.

BACKACHE

As your abdomen enlarges, and your center of gravity shifts, you may experience some sporadic back pain. If you suddenly feel a different type of backache or spasm, and no matter what you do, you can't relieve it, you should alert your doctor. It could be anything from simple back strain to a kidney infection to the onset of premature labor. As soon as your back starts to ache, start monitoring for contractions. If your abdomen is quiet, it is probably not a sign of labor, but of some other problem. Whatever it is, you will probably need to be seen by your doctor if the pain persists for more than twenty-four hours.

CHILLS, FEVER

You may think that it's just a cold, and indeed, it may be just a cold. To be on the safe side, call your doctor anyway, because it could also be a sign of any number of medical problems, including kidney infection and flu.

DIARRHEA, INTESTINAL CRAMPS

Maybe it was the Chinese food you had last night, but at this stage of pregnancy, diarrhea or cramps could also indicate the onset of premature labor. The same hormone that triggers labor can also cause diarrhea. Your best bet is to call your doctor and to check for other signs of preterm labor.

NAGGING FEELING THAT SOMETHING ISN'T RIGHT

When it comes to the health and well-being of their children, some mothers seem to have a sixth sense, intuitively guessing when something is wrong. While it's true that some women may just be overly anxious, I feel that it's important to report these feelings to your physician or health care practitioner. First, if nothing is wrong, your mind will be put to rest. Second, upon examination, your doctor or midwife may be able to detect if there are any problems brewing.

Highlights of the Second Trimester: Fourteen through Twenty-six Weeks

During these thirteen weeks, your baby is growing by leaps and bounds. By the end of the fourth month, he may be twice as long and six times as heavy as he was at the start of the trimester!

Early in the second trimester, your baby develops hair and eyebrows. His body is encased in a greasy covering called the vernix caseosa, which scientists suspect may protect the fetus from continual exposure to the amniotic fluid. He may also be covered with lanugo, or fine hair. Buds for teeth start to form. The baby is now kicking, grasping, and sucking. Between the sixteenth and twentieth weeks, his digestive tract is undergoing the process of becoming mechanically and chemically functional and his swallowing reflex is well developed. By the eighteenth or twentieth week, you begin to feel that something really is living inside of you.

By five months, the placenta and the umbilical cord are fully operational. With the help of a doppler, an ultrasound device, you and your doctor can hear the baby's heartbeat. At the end of the second trimester, your baby weights about 1.5 pounds and is about 14 inches long.

Third Trimester

What's Normal and Why It's Happening

FATIGUE, DIFFICULTY SLEEPING

By the third trimester, many women begin to wish that the whole thing was already over. You're probably getting mentally and physically tired of being pregnant. Your body is working overtime, both nourishing the new life and carrying around the extra weight. To make matters worse, hormonal changes, and the simple fact that you may not be able to find a comfortable position in bed, often result in restless nights. If you're carrying a "night owl," his or her increased activity after dark may make it hard for you to rest. If you can, try catching a nap during the day to compensate for sleep loss at night. At the very least, put your feet up and relax for at least fifteen minutes several times a day.

AWKWARDNESS

Your center of gravity has shifted, which makes simple tasks, like stepping down from a curb or getting up from a chair, more difficult. Wear low-heeled shoes and be especially careful walking up and down stairs or getting out of the tub, two places where accidents often happen. On really icy, slippery days, stay indoors.

FREQUENT URINATION

Hormonal changes kept you running to the bathroom in the first trimester. Now, pressure on the bladder from the growing uterus may also be causing increased urination. Some women may feel the urge to urinate, but have difficulty passing urine. To facilitate urination, support your abdomen in your hands while sitting on the toilet.

INCREASE IN BRAXTON HICKS CONTRACTIONS

Sometime in your eighth or ninth month, you may experience an increase in Braxton Hicks contractions. These contractions, as previously mentioned, are usually painless and do not develop into labor. For a few seconds, you may feel a stiffening or hardening of the uterus. When the contraction is over, the uterus softens. BRAXTON HICKS CONTRACTIONS ARE IRREGULAR AND INFREQUENT. If you notice an unusual amount of uterine activity, or have more than four contractions in an hour, call your doctor.

CONSTIPATION

For many women, constipation becomes more of a problem in the third trimester. As the digestive system continues to slow down, bowel movements may become more infrequent, contributing to any bloatedness or discomfort you may already be feeling. To avoid constipation, make sure you get some exercise daily (a walk at a comfortable pace may do the trick), drink plenty of fluids, and increase your consumption of fruits, vegetables, and whole grains.

SHORTNESS OF BREATH

The flight of steps you once sailed up with ease has now become as burdensome as Mount Everest. Obviously, the weight gain has something to do with this. In addition, the uterus may be pressing against the lungs, hampering your ability to breath deeply.

BIZARRE DREAMS OR NIGHTMARES, FANTASIES, ABSENTMINDEDNESS

Many women report having strange dreams throughout pregnancy, particularly in the last trimester. Some women report an increase in sexual dreams. Other typical dreams reflect concern about the health of the baby or fears about getting through labor or coping with parenthood. Although some of these dreams may be disturbing, they are not premonitions, but a normal outlet for whatever fears you may be experiencing. After all, the third trimester is a time when you may have a lot on your mind. For many women, the anticipation of labor can be almost as bad as the experience itself. If you work full-time and are planning to return to work after the baby is born, you may be concerned about finding childcare and handling the dual responsibility of family and career. If you already have children, you may be worried about how the new arrival will disrupt your family. If you've suffered the tragedy of stillbirth or are fearful of premature birth, this can be an anxiety-provoking time. Once again, talking about your fears with other women who understand what you're going through can make a real difference in your outlook.

LEG CRAMPS

As any pregnant woman can tell you, there's nothing worse than being jolted out of a sound sleep by the throbbing pain of a leg cramp. Other than getting adequate exercise to promote circulation, there's little you can do to prevent leg cramps. Sometimes cramping is a sign of a calcium deficiency and if the problem becomes severe, your doctor may prescribe a supplement. Severe leg cramps may also indicate an intolerance to milk products, in which case your doctor will omit them from your diet and prescribe a calcium supplement.

HEMORRHOIDS

Hemorrhoid discomfort may intensify due to increased uterine pressure on the rectum. Try to improve the condition by adding bran, fruits, and vegetables to your diet, and by spending more time off your feet.

VARICOSE VEINS

Varicose veins are caused by the increased burden being placed on your circulatory system by the expansion of the maternal blood supply. At this point in your pregnancy, avoid standing on your feet for long periods of time or sitting in a cross-legged position, which can hamper circulation. Rest with your feet up whenever you get the chance and try to take a brisk walk each day to improve circulation.

INDIGESTION, HEARTBURN, DIFFICULTY GETTING THROUGH A MEAL

During the last trimester, indigestion and heartburn often become chronic and very annoying problems. Heartburn occurs when the acid used to digest food, normally found in the stomach, flows back into the esophagus, causing the burning sensation. Some women find it helpful not to drink liquids with their meals, and to sit upright for at least forty-five minutes after eating. If heartburn interferes with sleep, try propping extra pillows under your head to elevate the top portion of your body. As the uterus gets bigger, you're liable to feel quite "crowded" in your abdominal area. Eating a big meal in one sitting may be impossible. Instead, try to eat several minimeals throughout the day.

BACK STRAIN

You may be heavier than you ever were in your entire life, and to make matters worse, your back-breaking load is unevenly distributed, throwing off your posture. It's no wonder that so many pregnant women complain of back strain. Mild exercises can help, especially those that gently stretch and relax those overworked muscles. However, any change in back pain should be reported to your doctor.

INCREASED FETAL ACTIVITY

As the fetus grows and becomes more active, you will become more aware of the fact that a new life has temporarily taken up residence in your body. You may also notice that certain activities, like eating, exercise, or listening to music, seem to elicit more response than others.

What's Not Normal and What It May Mean

UNTIL THE THIRTY-SEVENTH WEEK, IT IS NOT NORMAL TO HAVE FOUR OR MORE REGULAR CONTRACTIONS AN HOUR

Four or more contractions an hour is a sign of labor. Some contractions are painful, but others are painless, and unless you are carefully monitoring abdominal activity, you may be having contractions and not even know it. In fact, any time you notice a sudden increase in contractions, you should carefully evaluate whether you may be experiencing other signs of pre-term labor, such as backache, menstrual-type cramps, diarrhea, or pelvic pressure. IF YOU SUSPECT THAT YOU MAY BE HEADED FOR PRETERM LABOR, CALL YOUR DOCTOR IMMEDIATELY. You may be a candidate for home uterine monitoring. Ask your doctor.

SUDDEN CHANGE IN FETAL ACTIVITY

By this time, especially in the latter half of this trimester, you should be aware of any pattern in fetal activity. For example, if your baby is exceptionally active after you eat or exercise, and suddenly you notice that he's not, there's no need to panic—he may just be sleeping—but you should be aware of his movements for the next few hours. Try doing things that normally elicit a strong reaction, like exercising or listening to loud music. If you don't feel any movement over a four-hour period, call your doctor to be on the safe side. Also call your doctor if you notice a dramatic decline in fetal movement. For instance, if over a two-day period, a normally active baby suddenly seems to be sluggish and slow, you should also notify your doctor. A change in fetal activity doesn't necessarily mean that your baby is in trouble. However, it could be an early-warning sign of a possible complication such as a placental problem or a maternal illness that is preventing the baby from getting adequate nourishment. This last could result in an undergrown, inactive baby who may be headed for stillbirth. Rest assured that even if there is a potential threat to your pregnancy, your doctor will in all likelihood have ample time to do something about it. Much can be done to improve the womb environment. If it is late enough in the pregnancy, and the condition is extremely severe, your doctor has the option of delivering the baby so he can be treated in an intensive care nursery.

GUSH OR TRICKLE OF FLUID FROM VAGINA

As your baby gets bigger and stronger, he may give a sudden kick to the bladder that could result in the involuntary release of urine. However, a gush of fluid could also mean that you're leaking amniotic fluid or that your membranes have ruptured. If the fluid has a yellowish or greenish color, be sure to tell your doctor, because it could be a sign of meconium—fecal waste from the baby's bowels—which is passed by the baby during stress. No matter what you think it may be, let your doctor know if you leak fluid.

CHANGE IN BACK PAIN

As your abdomen grows bigger, you may be experiencing back strain. If you notice a change in back pain, especially in the lower back, it could be a sign of preterm labor. Be careful to check for other symptoms, such as contractions, menstrual-type cramps, and pelvic pressure. Let your doctor know about the back pain so he can evaluate the situation.

SUDDEN SWELLING OR EDEMA

During the last trimester in particular a woman must be careful to watch for the symptoms of preeclampsia. As we all should know by now, sudden swelling, especially in the hands, feet, and face, is a red flag that should not be ignored. If you notice swelling, call your doctor. It's also a good idea to check your blood pressure to make sure that you are not hypertensive, another symptom of preeclampsia.

MENSTRUAL-TYPE CRAMPS

At this late stage, menstrual-type cramps could indicate the onset of preterm labor, especially if they are accompanied by other symptoms, including pelvic pressure, low back pain, or diarrhea.

DIARRHEA, CRAMPS

You may think you have a stomach virus, but diarrhea is a classic sign of labor. Don't ignore it. Call your doctor for advice.

SPOTTING OR BLEEDING

By now, you should know to call your doctor at the first sign of blood. Bleeding or spotting could indicate placental problems, such as placenta previa or an abruption or separation. It could also be a sign of infection.

CHANGE IN VAGINAL DISCHARGE

If you notice a thicker-than-usual discharge or one that is foul-smelling, call your doctor. It could be a sign of infection. A mucusy discharge could be a sign of an incompetent cervix, which could lead to preterm labor.

FEVER OR CHILLS

Fever and chills could be a sign of maternal infection or of an infection of the amniotic fluid. Call your doctor immediately.

BURNING SENSATION WHILE URINATING, CLOUDY URINE, BLOOD IN URINE

Any one of these symptoms could be a sign of a vaginal or kidney infection. However, the bleeding could also be from the pregnancy, as in the case of placenta previa. Needless to say, call your doctor.

POOR WEIGHT GAIN

If you're not gaining a pound a week on average, or if you begin to lose weight, notify your doctor. This could indicate an undergrown baby that is malnourished or other problems.

EXCESSIVE WEIGHT GAIN

Many people treat weight gain during pregnancy as a joke and attribute a sudden increase in weight to the legendary insatiable appetite of a mother-to-be. However, excessive weight gain is no laughing matter. A gain of more than two pounds per week could be a sign of a problem such as pre-eclampsia or diabetes. If you're putting on more weight than you should, call your doctor.

Third-Trimester Highlights

At the beginning of the third trimester, your baby is still totally dependent on you for survival. He cannot breathe on his own, nor can he obtain proper nourishment outside of you. By the end of this three-month period, however, your baby should be prepared to leave the protective environment of the womb, capable of performing all critical life functions.

Your baby now weighs between 2 and 3 pounds. He is beginning to shed the lanugo, the fine hair or down that covers his body. His eyebrows and eyelashes have grown in, and his eyes are a dark gray. As he begins to store fat beneath his skin, his color changes from a reddish hue to one more representative of his final skin color. By now, your baby has become more aware of outside stimuli, and may respond to light, sound, and pain.

Although your baby is not yet capable of breathing, he may be exercising his lungs by making slight breathing movements. If the amniotic fluid passes into his trachea, he may start to hiccup. Some women may experience this as a slight pulsating movement every few seconds in their abdomen.

By the end of the seventh month, your baby stands a good chance of survival if born prematurely and cared for in a skilled intensive care nursery. (Whenever I tell this to expectant mothers, I'm always quick to add that the best neonatal nursery of all—the womb—has been provided free of charge by God, and no matter how technologically sophisticated an artificial environment may be, it can't compete with a mother.)

Your baby's brain develops rapidly during the eighth month, one of the reasons why good nutrition is so important during this critical period.

As your baby gets bigger—he is gaining on average 1 ounce per day—you both may feel more crowded. If your baby is pressing against your stomach or other digestive organs, you may be unable to eat a big meal in one sitting. Your growing baby, in turn, is no longer able to move freely in the amniotic fluid. Instead of the gentle movements you may have once felt, at this stage of pregnancy you may feel a quick jab or punch as your baby strains for space.

By the ninth month, your baby's lungs should be fully matured and your baby already has hair, long fingernails, and dark gray eyes. At this point, your baby may become engaged, that is, he may descend into the pelvis, ready for birth. Ideally, the baby presents in the headfirst or vertex position. Sometimes, however, a baby may try to enter the world in the breech or rear-first position, and some may present transverse or shoulder first. These babies will often shift into the correct position before delivery, on their own or with a little help from a knowledgeable doctor or midwife. If not, in some but certainly not all cases, a cesarean may be necessary.

By the thirty-seventh week, or the end of the ninth month, your baby should be ready for life in the outside world.

S I X

Your Home-Care Program

There's a lot more to good prenatal care than simply visiting your doctor every three or four weeks and giving little thought to your pregnancy in between. As the twenty-four-hour-a-day caregiver of your pregnancy, you need to stay in constant touch with your body. If a potential problem arises, you can't afford to wait until your next doctor's appointment to find out what's wrong. You and your doctor need to know about it immediately. That is why I prescribe this simple, easy-to-follow program for all of my patients. I urge every pregnant woman to set aside a specific time each day to take stock of her pregnancy and to collect vital information that could prevent a crisis from happening in the first place.

First Half of Pregnancy

Daily Weight Gain or Loss

Monitoring weight gain or loss is one of the most important things you can do during pregnancy, and yet many women are reluctant to step on the scale between visits to the doctor for fear of finding out something they really don't want to know. This is a mistake. During these early months, it's important that a mother-to-be restrict her weight gain to under 5 pounds. If she doesn't, she may be forced to choose between cutting back on food in the second half of the pregnancy when the baby needs it the most, or gaining so much weight that she puts herself and the baby at risk of serious medical complications.

It is also important that the mother not lose any weight, either, so she can build up her reserves of essential nutrients. This is no easy task for the woman who is suffering from severe nausea and, consequently, may be unable to eat enough to support her own needs and that of the new life within her. If the mother is concerned that she is not eating enough, she should check with her doctor.

WEIGH YOURSELF EVERY DAY.   In any trimester, a gain of more than two pounds a week should be reported to your doctor. A weight loss of more than two pounds per week should also be reported, especially if you suspect you are not meeting your nutritional needs. However, if you are carrying twins, you may need to gain more weight. Be sure to talk to your doctor about your increased nutritional needs.

Check Blood Pressure Weekly

Hypertension can be a serious problem in pregnancy and it can also be a symptom of other complications. The quicker we can detect and treat high blood pressure, the less chance it has of adversely affecting the health of the mother or baby. Therefore, I believe all pregnant women—especially those who are considered "high risk"—should monitor their own blood pressure between visits to their doctor or midwife. An inexpensive blood pressure gauge can be purchased at almost any drugstore.

For most nonpregnant women, a measure of 120/80 is considered normal, although there may be slight variations. The 120 measures the pressure in the arteries when the heart is contracting, or the systolic pressure. The 80 represents the pressure in the arteries when the heart is relaxed, or the diastolic pressure.

Typically, blood pressure during pregnancy is slightly lower than normal, which may cause some drowsiness and light-headedness.

BLOOD PRESSURE SHOULD BE MEASURED WEEKLY. On that day, take your blood pressure once upon rising and once before retiring at night. A change in either the diastolic or systolic measure of ten units or more from week to week or morning to night should be reported to your doctor.

Starting the Second Half of Pregnancy

Checking for Contractions

Premature labor rarely strikes without any advance notice. Unfortunately, many women are unaware of the warning signs and wait until it's too late to do anything about it before alerting their doctors. One of the warning signs of labor is the onset of contractions. Often these contractions are painless, and unless you are deliberately looking for them, they will very likely pass unnoticed until you experience other symptoms of labor. For this reason, I urge all pregnant women to check for labor contractions at least twice a day, for a half-hour period at a time. (Morning and evening may be the most convenient times.) You can do this by yourself, or you can enlist the support of your spouse. Lie down and put your fingertips on your abdomen. If you feel a tightening and then a softening, you are probably feeling a contraction. If you feel more than two of these in a half-hour period, continue to monitor for another half hour. If you have more than four an hour, call your doctor for further instructions. He may want to see you, especially if you are having other symptoms that could indicate the onset of labor, or he may want you to continue to monitor for a few more hours to see if the contractions are occurring with any regularity.

As you become more aware of your body, you may notice that some activities, such as climbing steps or driving, may bring on contractions. An occasional increase in contractions over a short period of time is no cause for alarm. However, if you find that some activities always bring you to the danger point—that is, more than four contractions an hour—avoid them as much as possible.

Checking for Fetal Activity

Terror hit us three weeks before my due date. I could not get my baby to move. He had been very quiet in terms of movement throughout the entire pregnancy, but this was extreme. No matter how I moved or how we prodded and poked, we could not get any movement. I called Dr. Sem and he said he would meet us at the hospital. Then in the car on the way over to the hospital, I felt one large thump. I remember feeling silly for my fears, but I kept thinking and decided one kick didn't mean much if he was becoming entangled in the umbilical cord. We had come so far and it had taken too many years; a loss now would have been unbearable. Once in the hospital and hooked up to the monitors we found out that everything was going to be fine.

— Kelly, two previous losses, six years' infertility, gave birth to healthy son

Most doctors tell you to watch for movement, and of course, everyone is thrilled when you finally feel the baby kick. What they don't tell you is that there should be a certain amount of movement, and if you suddenly don't feel anything, it could be a sign that your baby is in trouble. My baby had a pattern of moving every three hours. When she didn't, I knew that something was wrong.

— Roberta, three miscarriages, delivered a full-term healthy baby

The first time you feel your baby move can be one of the most exciting moments of your life. For about twenty weeks, you've put up with many of the minor and sometimes major inconveniences of pregnancy, and now your vigilance is beginning to pay off. From now on, you will be in constant communication with your baby.

Fetal movement is not only a reassuring reminder that all of the fatigue and heartburn is for a worthy cause, it can also provide valuable clues that in some cases could save the life of your unborn child. A baby that is beginning to fail due to placental problems or maternal illness may begin to show signs of slowing down. Unfortunately, due to a lack of education, most women fail to take advantage of this important source of information.

Although I recognize the valuable contribution technology has made to childbirth, I know that in my practice, it is usually not a sophisticated ultrasound or an electronic monitor that first detects a potential problem; it is an observant mother who has noticed that her typically active baby has become unusually quiet. If she brings this information to my attention early enough, before a little problem can grow into a full-blown emergency, then in most cases we can take the appropriate steps to avert a crisis.

Although it is especially critical for high-risk patients to become expert in monitoring fetal movement, I feel it is easy enough for any woman to do and in many cases, it will be well worth the effort.

From the first time you feel fetal movement (at around the twentieth week after the last menstrual cycle or the eighteenth week of gestation) until delivery, it is important to watch for any significant changes in activity. However, before you can discern any changes, you must be extremely familiar with your baby's pattern of movement. Therefore, I advise my patients to keep a little notebook with them during the day (hopefully, you and the baby are sleeping at night!) and to jot down the times when your baby appears to be the most active. For instance, many women report a sudden surge of activity after a big meal or late in the afternoon on the way home from work. Some babies may sleep soundly all afternoon, in which case there will be no activity, but at night it may feel as if they're doing aerobics!

In about two to four weeks, you will begin to detect a pattern. If you notice any deviation from the normal pattern, it doesn't necessarily mean that anything is wrong, but it is a sign that you should be somewhat more observant than usual.

If after a four-hour period, you fail to detect any of the usual movement, try doing some activities that generally elicit a response: Lie down, have something to eat, turn on some loud music. If nothing happens, call your doctor.

If a woman is carrying twins, she must work doubly hard to keep track of both babies. She must not only locate the positions of the two fetuses, but she must also learn to differentiate each one's movements. In about 10 percent of all cases involving twins in utero, one twin thrives while the other is smaller and undergrown. Why does this happen? In the uterus, the babies are competing for the same space and nourishment. In some cases, one twin may get more than the other. Therefore, it's important for the mother who is carrying twins to recognize if one baby is beginning to show signs of malnutrition or distress.

Whether you're carrying one or two (or more) babies, keep in mind that a slump in activity doesn't necessarily mean that anything is the matter. Quite possibly, your baby may have changed his sleeping schedule without letting you know (something he will do from time to time after he's born, too). However, since it could also be a warning sign that something is beginning to go wrong, it's best to pass this information on to your doctor.

After Twenty-eight Weeks

Identifying Fetal Position

By twenty-eight weeks, you should not only be familiar with your baby's activity pattern, but should also take note of your baby's position. Ideally, you should be feeling movement toward the top of your belly, which means that the baby is in the correct head-down or vertex position. However, if you feel more activity toward the bottom of your belly near your bladder, and you find that you frequently have to urinate after the baby moves, chances are the baby is in the breech or rear-first position, increasing your risk of cesarean delivery. Some babies may shift to the correct position on their own, but some may need a little help. A doctor may try to turn the baby through external manipulation. This procedure may be performed safely up until the thirty-fourth week. After that, it is more difficult to perform due to the increased size of the fetus and the decreased amount of amniotic fluid, and could result in fetal injury or even bring on labor. Obviously, if an attempt is made to shift the fetal position, the mother must be closely monitored and given medication to keep the uterus quiet.

The mother-to-be can also perform a simple exercise at home to encourage a breech baby to turn around. Three times a day (always before meals to avoid indigestion or heartburn), for about ten minutes at a time, she should kneel and lower her chest to the floor, rear end up. In many cases, within a few weeks she will notice a change in the location of fetal activity. Once the baby has turned, she should discontinue the exercise or the baby could turn back.

In some cases, no matter what you or your doctor does, the baby will not turn to the vertex position prior to delivery. Depending on the baby's position and the skill of the doctor, you may or may not require a cesarean.

Taking Care of Yourself

With many women today holding down two full-time jobs— one at home and the other at the workplace—it's difficult under the best of circumstances to find the time to eat properly and get enough exercise and relaxation. In many cases, it doesn't matter if you routinely skip lunch to meet deadlines at work or cut back on your sleep to catch up on housekeeping. However, it's a different story during pregnancy. A stressful lifestyle that results in poor eating habits and lack of sleep will not only add to your fatigue, but could harm your growing baby. To ensure a successful pregnancy, the expectant mother must make a commitment to take good care of herself. No matter what her other responsibilities may be, the mother-to-be must make sure that she takes the time to eat well and get enough rest. She should also try to avoid stressful situations, either at work or at home. To keep in the best physical shape possible, she should try to engage in some kind of moderate exercise several times a week. (Before doing any exercise during pregnancy, check with your doctor.)

Pregnancy is the time to be a little bit selfish. Remember, you are responsible not only for your own health and well-being but also for that of your developing baby.

The following information will help you plan for a healthy and happy pregnancy.

Good Nutrition: Building a Firm Foundation

During the miracle of pregnancy, a tiny egg—so small that you can barely see it with the naked eye—unites with a microscopic sperm to become a full-grown baby. Throughout the nine-month gestation period, this growing new life relies solely on the mother to meet its nutritional needs. The mother must not only provide for the increased demands that pregnancy places on her body, but she must also make sure that her baby is getting enough nutrients to develop normally.

Poor maternal nutrition at the beginning of pregnancy can have an adverse affect on the development of the embryo, leading to miscarriage or birth defects. Although most of us don't have to worry about malnutrition—Americans on average take in too many, not too few, calories—we do have to worry about our intake of certain nutrients.

Many of us have hectic lifestyles. Too often we skip meals or eat them on the run. Soda, french fries, and candy bars are high in calories, but low in nutrients. Therefore, it's really ironic that at the same time many of us were filling up on junk food, calories became a national obsession. Today, many women of childbearing age are so accustomed to eating junk food while being so preoccupied with losing weight that they bounce back and forth from fat food to fad diet. In fact, studies reveal that many women in their late teens and early twenties have eating disorders that are seriously compromising their health. Although they may shed pounds, they are also depleting their reserves of vital nutrients such as iron, folic acid, and calcium. In pregnancy, these and other nutrients are critical to the growth and development of the baby. A woman and her growing child are at a disadvantage if her body stores are depleted.

A good, well-balanced diet before and during pregnancy is the best way to ensure that the new life will get adequate nourishment. If at all possible, a woman should embark on a pregnancy from a position of strength. If you haven't already developed good eating habits, part of your pregnancy planning should include putting yourself on a healthy, well-rounded diet.

During pregnancy, most doctors prescribe special prenatal vitamin supplements to compensate for the increased demand for various vitamins and minerals. I feel that it's also important for women to take a good multivitamin before pregnancy. Studies have shown that taking a multivitamin for at least one month prior to conception and throughout early pregnancy greatly reduces the risk of having a baby with anencephaly, a neural tube defect in which the baby is missing all or part of his brain and would have no chance of survival, or spina bifida, an opening in the spinal column that can be life-threatening. If you're not taking a multivitamin already, ask your doctor to recommend one.

IF YOU'RE UNDERWEIGHT

Women who are significantly underweight at the start of a pregnancy—at least 15 percent below ideal body weight—run a greater risk of producing low-birth-weight or premature infants. Premature and low-birth-weight babies—babies 5½ pounds or under at birth—are at risk of any number of life-threatening problems, including difficulty breathing during and after delivery and hypoglycemia (low blood sugar).

Ideally, underweight women should try to put on extra weight prior to pregnancy. They should talk to their doctors or qualified nutritionists about a weight-gain diet. One word of caution: Don't try to make up those pounds by consuming vast amounts of empty calories or junk food. An underweight woman needs to build up her reserves of essential nutrients so that her supplies are replenished during her baby's critical growth periods. In preparation for pregnancy, her diet should emphasize foods rich in calcium, iron, and folic acid.

If you're beginning your pregnancy underweight, don't worry, you can make up for lost time. Your doctor will probably recommend a high-calorie diet, as well as one for greater-than-usual weight gain.

IF YOU'RE OVERWEIGHT

If you're overweight—that is, 20 percent above what the insurance charts say you should weigh—there's nothing more depressing than contemplating putting on more weight during pregnancy. No matter how heavy you may be, pregnancy is not the time to diet. In fact, you will still need to gain an additional 15 pounds or more to ensure adequate growth and nutrition for your child.

As we've seen earlier, maternal obesity can lead to a number of serious complications in pregnancy, including gestational diabetes, hypertension, and macrosomia (an abnormally enlarged baby). If you're thinking about becoming pregnant, your first inclination may be to go on a crash diet. That would be a mistake. Sudden weight loss can throw off your hormonal balance, making it difficult or even impossible to conceive. In addition, a deprivation-type diet is probably not well balanced and would not provide enough of the essential vitamins and nutrients you'll need later on.

If you want to lose weight before pregnancy, you must give yourself enough time. Follow a sensible, well-rounded diet plan with the goal of losing a pound or two a week until you reach your desired weight. After taking off the weight, stick to a sensible maintenance diet until pregnancy. Once you're pregnant, follow the standard pregnancy diet, returning to your maintenance diet after you stop breast-feeding.

Pregnancy is not the time to lose weight—if you stay within the normal guidelines the extra pounds are put to good use—

and it should not be a time of permanent weight gain, either. However, for many women, it is. With each pregnancy, the average woman gains seven pounds that she never loses. Obviously, the woman who begins pregnancy overweight has the added burden of having even more weight to lose after pregnancy. For their own health, and the health of their babies, I urge my patients to try, if at all possible, to attain a normal, healthy weight before becoming pregnant.

Once she becomes pregnant, an expectant mother needs to consume an additional 80,000 calories to sustain a pregnancy from conception to delivery. That means the average pregnant woman must consume about 300 more calories a day than she normally would to maintain her prepregnancy weight. (If she's underweight, she may have to eat more, and if she's overweight, she may have to eat less.)

At one time, probably when many of your mothers were pregnant, doctors were very strict about weight gain during pregnancy, advising women not to gain an ounce over twenty pounds. Many doctors believed that a weight gain beyond this amount would result in a large baby that would be difficult to deliver and would also put the mother at risk of obesity after pregnancy. Today, we view things differently. We now believe that the optimum weight gain during pregnancy is anywhere between 24 and 28 pounds for women of normal weight, 30 pounds for underweight women, and about 15 pounds for overweight women.

The following chart shows that the additional weight is put to good use.

Pounds to Grow On	
Fetus	7.5 lbs
Amniotic fluid	2 lbs
Placenta	1.5 lbs
Uterus	2 lbs
Increase in mother's blood volume	3 lbs
Increased breast size	1 lb
Fluid retention	4 lbs
Maternal fat	7 lbs
	28 lbs

Inadequate weight gain can cause severe problems for the developing baby. During World War II, when famine struck various countries, sometimes for months at a time, pregnant women were forced to subsist on 1,000 calories a day with a meager 30–40 grams of protein, not quite half of the recommended amount. Their babies paid dearly for their mothers' poor nutrition. The rate of stillbirths and congenital malformations soared for infants conceived during famine, and average birth weights dropped dramatically, especially for women who were malnourished during the latter half of pregnancy.

The tragic outcome of many pregnancies during times of war and famine underscores the importance of good nutrition for expectant mothers. What you eat—the quantity and quality of food—and at which stage of the pregnancy you eat it, can have a dramatic impact on your health and the health of the baby.

Loading up on fattening, low-nutrient junk food early in pregnancy can cause a rapid weight gain at a time when the mother least needs it. In the second half of pregnancy, a woman who has already gained a substantial amount of weight may feel compelled to cut back at a time when the fetus most needs the extra nutrients, thus endangering the health of the baby.

To avoid the "feast/famine syndrome," a pregnant woman must be especially careful about the pattern of weight gain. Ideally, she should gain between 2 and 5 pounds in the first trimester, and after that, about one pound a week or 3 to 4 pounds a month until delivery. While weight gain may fluctuate slightly from woman to woman, the overall trend of weight gain should be similar. (As I noted in the pregnancy-monitoring section in chapter 5, a gain of over 2 pounds per week should be reported to your doctor.)

MAKE EVERY CALORIE COUNT

Simply increasing your daily caloric intake by 300 calories during pregnancy is not enough. Pregnant women need greater quantities of specific nutrients to adjust to the physiological changes that occur in their bodies during pregnancy and for the health and well-being of their babies.

Protein   Pregnant women require at least 75 grams of protein a day, almost double the amount needed by nonpregnant adults. Since the typical American diet is too high in protein to begin with, often little adjustment must be made during pregnancy. (Women who consume little meat and dairy products, such as those from low socioeconomic groups or vegetarians, may need to increase their protein consumption.)

High-quality protein, which is easily absorbed by the body, is found in abundance in meat, fish, dairy products, and eggs. Poorer quality protein (which is more difficult to absorb) is found in legumes, nuts, vegetables, and grains, and is better utilized when consumed in combination with high-quality proteins.

Protein is absorbed better when eaten in several small helpings rather than in one or two sittings. In fact, throughout your pregnancy, you'll feel more energetic and be better nourished if you avoid big meals and stick to six minimeals scattered throughout the day.

Iron   Iron is an essential component of hemoglobin, which is found in red blood cells. During pregnancy, when maternal blood volume grows dramatically, there is an increased demand for additional iron to provide for the synthesis of red blood cells. The mother suffers more from an inadequate supply of this nutrient than the baby, who will "rob" from maternal stores if he's not getting enough from the mother's blood supply. As a result, iron deficiency can lead to maternal anemia, causing the mother-to-be to feel even more draggy and fatigued than she normally would. A lack of iron can also cause a decreased tolerance for blood loss during pregnancy and a greater susceptibility to infection.

A pregnant woman needs 30 to 60 mg of iron a day to ensure that there will be enough on hand for her own needs and those of her baby. Although most prenatal vitamins contain an adequate amount of iron, it's still important to include iron-rich foods in your diet.

Foods rich in iron include liver, red meat, dark green vegetables, and whole grains. Iron in food is better absorbed if taken along with a vitamin C source at the same meal, such as orange juice or broccoli.

Many women, especially those who entered pregnancy with low iron reserves, are given iron supplements during pregnancy to ensure an adequate level. Unfortunately, these supplements may cause nausea, diarrhea, or constipation. Since many women in the first trimester may already suffer from a host of gastrointestinal (GI) problems, doctors often wait until the second trimester—when the need for iron is the greatest—to prescribe the additional iron. Many women have found that iron goes down more easily if taken with meals. The only drawback is that it may not be absorbed as well, but taking iron with meals is certainly preferable to not taking it at all.

Calcium Unless you regularly drink a quart of milk a day, during pregnancy you need to increase your daily calcium requirement by a whopping 50 percent, to 1,200 mg.

Although dairy products are the best source of calcium, this vital nutrient is also found in dark green vegetables, sardines with bones, and nuts. Since most maternal vitamin supplements only supply between 15 and 25 percent of the recommended daily allowance (RDA) for calcium, you better get used to drinking a lot of milk or eating dairy products such as cheese and yogurt.

If you fail to ingest enough calcium, your baby will get her share by depleting maternal bone stores of the nutrient, increasing your risk of developing osteoporosis later in life.

Calcium may also help normalize blood pressure. Some studies have found an association between inadequate calcium during pregnancy and the onset of hypertension.

If you're lactose intolerant, that is, have an adverse reaction to milk products, talk to your doctor about calcium supplementation. Calcium carbonate is the best because it is the most easily absorbed by the body.

Folic acid Folic acid plays an essential role in the production of DNA, the so-called building blocks of the body. The requirement for this essential nutrient doubles during pregnancy to 800 micrograms per day.

Folic acid deficiency, which can cause anemia, is the most

common nutrient deficiency during pregnancy. Fortunately, most prenatal vitamins include 100 percent of the RDA for folic acid. However, women with a history of placental separation (abrupto placentae) or epilepsy may require greater amounts of folic acid than other expectant mothers. These women should ask their doctors about taking a supplement and should eat foods rich in this vital nutrient.

Good nutritional sources include organ and other meats, dark green vegetables, eggs, orange juice, and whole grains.

Take note: Women who have used oral contraceptives may enter pregnancy with lower reserves of folic acid and may therefore be more likely to develop a deficiency. Talk to your doctor about additional supplements.

Copper and zinc   During pregnancy, blood levels of copper and zinc are two and half times higher than for nonpregnant women. Both these minerals not only play a critical role in the functioning of the body, but may also help prevent intrauterine infection and the premature rupture of membranes. In fact, according to one recent study, women with low plasma zinc levels are more likely to develop complications during pregnancy, including mild toxemia, vaginitis, and abnormal labor, than women with higher levels. Therefore, during pregnancy, women should be sure to increase their intake of both copper and zinc. However, it is not advisable to take any supplements without consulting your doctor, because intakes of many vitamins and minerals far above the daily requirements can be toxic. Your best bet is to get these minerals through your diet. The following list shows which foods are high in copper and zinc.

Zinc: Best Sources

Meat	Green beans
Nuts	Lima Beans
Eggs	Nonfat dried milk
Wheat germ	(in general, however,
Oysters	dairy products are not
Whole wheat	good sources of zinc)
Oats	
Lobster	

Copper: Best Sources

Liver	Mushrooms
Shellfish	Whole grain cereals
Nuts	Gelatin
Cocoa	Liver
Cherries	

And keep in mind . . .

Sodium At one time, doctors believed that restricting salt during pregnancy would prevent pregnancy-induced hypertension and edema. We now know that's not the case. If a woman is prone to develop hypertension, she will get it regardless of salt intake. Nevertheless, since a high-sodium diet may be associated with hypertension in some individuals, it's probably a good idea to keep salt use to moderate levels.

Cholesterol If you're health conscious, you may be worried about the fact that many of the foods recommended for pregnancy, such as eggs, dairy, and meat, are high in cholesterol. Let me put your fears to rest. During pregnancy, cholesterol levels drop for most women. It's the one time in your life you can eat an occasional slice of liver or an egg a day without having to worry about the consequences. There is one exception to the rule. The woman who is entering pregnancy with a serious cholesterol problem—that is, a blood cholesterol level of 240 or more—should seek her doctor's advice on setting safe limits.

Alcohol One of my patients recently asked me whether the glass of wine she had with dinner prior to learning she was pregnant could adversely affect her baby. I told her to stop worrying: It is extremely unlikely that one drink would cause any of the serious complications that are associated with moderate to heavy drinking during pregnancy. Studies have shown that excessive maternal drinking—three or more drinks per day—increases the risk of fetal alcohol syndrome, a disorder characterized by abnormalities of the eyes, nose, heart, central nervous system, and by possible growth retardation. While very few of us may drink that heavily—especially during pregnancy—the effects of moderate drinking are unclear. There have been some studies that suggest a correlation between occasional drinking and an increased incidence of spontaneous abortion, behavior dysfunction in children, and suboptimal mental or motor development in newborns. There is also some evidence that occasional binge drinking may be just as bad as or worse than moderate daily intake.

My advice is, don't drink unless you have to. At times, an obstetrician may advise a patient who is experiencing cramping or contractions to have a glass of wine to calm the uterus. In this instance, it is far better to have the drink than run the risk of premature labor. But unless you're under doctor's orders, it's safer to abstain.

Food additives   Whenever there's a major news story on yet another food additive or pollutant that has been found to cause cancer in laboratory rats, I sit back and wait for the phone to ring. Invariably, at least a dozen patients will call, concerned that the artificial sweetener in the diet soda they've been drinking or the insecticide used to spray the fruit they've been eating will somehow hurt their unborn child.

While I don't want to make light of these concerns, I do feel that they should be put in their proper perspective. In minute quantities—the amount of artificial sweetener in a glass of soda or in a diet ice cream—few ingredients are harmful to consume during pregnancy.

You might point out, as one of my patients recently did, that just about everything we eat could be potentially hazardous. Cattle may have been beefed up with DES, chickens are routinely fed antibiotics, fruits are sprayed with insecticides, milk and fish may contain harmful PCBs, and the list goes on and on. While this all may be true, in all likelihood the small concentrations of these potentially hazardous substances found in food will not hurt you or your baby. To be on the safe side, however, I advise patients to follow the advice often given by stockbrokers: When in doubt, spread the risk around.

If you crave a diet soda every now and then, alternate between those containing aspartame and those containing saccharin. If you're torn between the toxins in liver, the growth hormones in beef, and the pollutants in fish, eat moderate amounts of each. In short, don't gorge on any one food.

If you live in a community with a specific problem—for instance, a water supply tainted by industrial waste or an unusually high concentration of PCBs in local fish—simply eliminate the offending substance from your diet. Switch to bottled water or eat canned fish from safer waters. In most cases, however, a sensible, well-balanced diet will be your best protection against the possible hazards lurking in the food or water supply.

DR. SEMCHYSHYN'S RECOMMENDATIONS FOR
DIET SUPPLEMENTATION

In addition to eating a well-balanced diet and taking a prenatal vitamin, I advise my patients to add the following to their diets. Check with your doctor before taking these or any other vitamin supplements during pregnancy.

1. *One carton of yogurt daily or two acidophilus pills twice a day.* The live, active cultures in yogurt create a climate that helps fight the spread of infection throughout the body. During pregnancy, women should consume at least one container of yogurt daily (flavored or unflavored) to benefit from this added protection. Any brand will do as long as the label states the stuff is made from live, active cultures. (The new yogurt snacks that come in cans should be avoided, since they do not contain live cultures.)

There are other good reasons to eat yogurt, including the fact that it is an excellent source of calcium and protein.

If you absolutely can't stand the flavor of yogurt, acidophilus pills (also known as yogurt pills) offer many of the same benefits. *Lactobacillus acidophilus,* or acidophilus, is a very effective source of friendly intestinal bacteria that help combat infection. Acidophilus pills can be bought at most pharmacies or health food stores.

2. *Vitamin C, 500 mg.* Due to hormonal changes during pregnancy, your gums can become tender and sore and may even bleed. Vitamin C helps heal and strengthen sore gums.

Therefore, I advise my patients to take an additional 500 mg of vitamin C daily.

An added bonus: Vitamin C also helps absorb iron, which is necessary for the production of red blood cells, and it may even lessen the severity of a cold if you do get one.

3. *Magnesium gluconate, 500 mg four times a day* (about 30 milligrams of elemental magnesium).   Magnesium is a mineral that helps the body cope with stress and is essential for nerve and muscle functioning. In cases of premature labor, high doses of magnesium are administered to relax uterine muscles and control contractions. Magnesium will also help reduce the indigestion that often accompanies pregnancy.

Although magnesium is found in a wide range of food, including nuts, leafy green vegetables, and figs, I believe that many diets are sorely lacking in this vital mineral. To make up for this loss, I recommend that my patients take an additional 500 mg of magnesium four times daily.

One word of caution: Avoid taking magnesium immediately after meals, since it neutralizes stomach acid and could interfere with digestion.

In the Workplace

If you're like most women these days, you're working at a job outside the home and you're planning to continue to work after the birth of your baby.

Unless you work for an unusually generous company, your pregnancy leave—assuming that you even get one—is probably around six weeks. Therefore, to maximize your time home with your baby, you're very likely planning to work as close to your delivery date as is within safe limits.

How long you can stay on the job depends on several factors, including the nature of your job, your overall health, and your mental outlook. Your doctor may suggest that you cease working earlier than you planned if your pregnancy has run into complications, or if you have a history of premature birth, are carrying more than one baby, or have an extremely long or stressful commute to work.

STRESS ON THE JOB

During pregnancy, your body is working overtime to maintain two lives: yours and your baby's. While some women may derive a great deal of satisfaction from their careers, it's important to remember that you stand a better chance of having a healthy, happy, and productive pregnancy if you don't continually push yourself to the point of exhaustion. If your job is very stressful, or if you're a very competitive person who just can't slow down, resign yourself to the fact that pregnancy is not the time to go for the big promotion or set any sales records.

Pregnancy is the time to pamper yourself, eat well, and get plenty of rest. Professional women—doctors, lawyers, nurses, MBAs—who are used to working twelve to sixteen hours a day should try to cut back to a more realistic eight or ten, and even less if it's necessary to preserve their health and sanity. Any woman who feels drained and depleted by the end of the day should consider reducing her hours or working part-time.

Even women with so-called high-risk or problem pregnancies may be able to stay on the job if they learn how to pace themselves and are pregnancy literate, that is, educated to watch for any signs of trouble. Cindy, a corporate attorney who ran into a number of complications during her pregnancy, including an incompetent cervix, partial placenta previa, and insulin-dependent diabetes, is a case in point. Considering her history, a doctor's first inclination might have been to prescribe bed rest until the baby was born. Cindy, however, was absolutely adamant that enforced rest would drive her crazy. I, too, believed that Cindy would fare better emotionally—and perhaps even physically—in a stimulating social environment rather than at home, alone all day, dwelling on her problems. I also knew that Cindy was one of my more knowledgeable patients, one who was very conscientious about her role as a partner in pregnancy. As soon as anything began to go wrong, I could count on Cindy to pick up the phone and call me.

Fortunately, Cindy and I were able to devise a pregnancy plan that enabled her to stay on the job. A combination of surgery to correct her weakened cervix, medication to control any uterine activity, and self-administered insulin shots twice a day to control her diabetes seemed to do the trick. In addition, for about a half hour every morning and afternoon at work, Cindy would wear a portable electronic monitor that measured uterine activity. Through telephone lines, the monitor was connected to a central nursing station that would detect any contractions. Working overtime was strictly forbidden and other than going out for an occasional dinner and a movie with her husband, Cindy promised to curtail her normally packed social calendar.

In her thirty-seventh week, on a Thursday afternoon, Cindy left work early because she went into labor. By Friday morning, she was the mother of a seven-pound son.

Not every woman will be able to overcome these kinds of complications and stay on the job. Not every woman will want to. However, it's comforting to know that for those who do, a combination of old-fashioned patient education and state-of-the-art medicine will make it possible for many of them to make it through pregnancy without forgoing the psychological or financial rewards of working.

WORK HAZARDS

Women who experience the greatest job stress of all are those who must worry about whether their work environment is harming their developing babies.

Certain jobs may indeed pose a greater risk of miscarriage and birth defects than others. In these cases, precautions must be taken to minimize the risks.

1. *Heavy physical work.*   Generally speaking, women in good health and with low-risk pregnancies who are accustomed to doing demanding physical work, such as lifting or carrying heavy objects, may continue to do so until the second half of pregnancy, as long as they follow certain guidelines.

Never pick up a heavy object when you are in a standing position, because it will place undue pressure on your abdomen. Lift from the lower part of your body by bending your knees and placing your weight over your legs. Protect your abdomen from any blows or injuries. Take frequent work and bathroom breaks. Drink plenty of fluids and keep some nourishing snacks at your work station. Most important, stop any activity as soon as you feel any strain or pain.

As your pregnancy progresses and your uterus expands,

you will very likely have to reduce your work hours or stop work earlier than if you had a less physically rigorous job. In some cases, an employer may be willing to transfer you to a less taxing position until after the pregnancy.

2. *Exposure to environmental hazards.* Job-related environmental hazards that may have a negative affect on a pregnancy include working with metals, certain chemicals, radiation, and even the video display terminal (VDT) that is fast replacing the typewriter in offices throughout the United States.

Exposure during pregnancy to heavy metals such as lead and mercury has been linked with miscarriage, stillbirth, mental retardation, and other birth defects. Women who work in factories or manufacturing plants where they are exposed to these substances should talk to their doctors, union representatives, and plant managers about the safety of remaining on the job. In many cases, industry or company guidelines will require a transfer to another job until after delivery.

Women in industrial or medical settings who are exposed to ionizing radiation or X rays should make sure that they stay well within the acceptable safety limits and should be meticulous about following safety protocol.

Although breathing in noxious fumes is something that no human being should have to endure, unfortunately industrial pollution is a fact of life. During the first trimester of pregnancy, women should especially avoid exposure to benzene (a known carcinogen), paint fumes, or other chemical vapors that could be harmful to fetal development.

If you're not sure about the safety of your workplace, your state health department or the federal Occupational Safety and Health Administration (OSHA) may be able to answer your questions. (See the appendix for details.)

VDTs: ARE THEY SAFE?

As computer terminals are fast becoming standard office equipment, pregnant women who spend their days toiling over VDTs are worried that the radiation emitted by these screens will somehow damage their babies.

Their concerns are understandable. In June 1988, a study released by researchers in California found that women who work more than twenty hours a week on VDTs are twice as likely to miscarry as those who don't.

Earlier animal studies have shown that cellular growth was disrupted in animal embryos exposed to the very low, frequent, pulsed nonionizing electromagnetic radiation emitted from VDTs.

After the release of the highly publicized California study, many employers and union officials reported that their pregnant office workers were being thrown into a panic. As the head of one union-sponsored health organization put it, "People imagine a little nuclear power plant zapping their baby." ("Pregnant Women Increasingly Fearful of VDTs," *The New York Times*, July 10, 1988.) Does this mean that as soon as a VDT operator gets pregnant she should quit her job and head for the hills? Not at all. Many scientists and doctors, including myself, feel that neither one of these studies conclusively proves that exposure to VDTs can adversely affect the outcome of a pregnancy.

In the California study, there are many factors that the researchers neglected to consider, including job-related stress, poor working conditions, and the accuracy with which women kept track of their actual time in front of the VDT.

As far as the animal studies are concerned, critics contend that these tests are also flawed because the radiation that was used is not identical to the type emitted by the VDTs. Until better studies are undertaken, the jury is still out on VDTs. We simply don't know to what extent, if any, exposure contributes to the likelihood of miscarriage.

To be on the safe side, I advise patients who must work on VDTs to limit their exposure to twenty hours a week or less if possible. In addition, since the amount of radiation emitted by VDTs is greater on the sides and backs of the terminals than directly in front of the screens, pregnant women should ask their employers to rearrange the workstations to minimize exposure to the backs and sides of nearby VDTs. In my experience, most employers are willing to accommodate their pregnant employees whenever they can. Cooperating with a valued worker not only makes it more likely she will return to her job after the birth of her child, but contributes to overall company morale. (For sources of more information on VDT safety, see the appendix.)

COMMUTING TO WORK

Some studies have shown that women who commute a great distance to work are at higher risk of premature labor than those who don't. As far as I'm concerned, however, the real culprit isn't the quantity, but the quality of the commute.

If it takes an hour or so to get to work, but you spend that time relaxing in air-conditioned comfort on a bus or in your car, there's no need to worry. If, however, your commute is especially stressful—if you're continually pushed and jostled on commuter trains or stuck for hours in aggravating touch-and-go traffic—you may want to stop working earlier or adjust your work schedule so you avoid the worst of the crowds. You might try working at home after hours.

A final word of caution. As your uterus enlarges and your center of gravity shifts, simple tasks like walking up a flight of steps or stepping off a curb must be undertaken with great care to avoid losing your balance, especially during rush hour. At 5:00 P.M., when everyone around you may be racing to catch a train or bail their car out of the parking lot, you must still tread slowly and carefully.

Sex: Is It Safe for High-Risk Mothers-to-Be?

In a normal, healthy pregnancy, couples can usually safely engage in sexual activity up until around the ninth month, unless the mother develops complications that could lead to miscarriage or premature birth. However, high-risk couples are usually told to abstain from sex altogether for the sake of the baby. Period. End of discussion.

I can understand why doctors treating high-risk couples—and even the couples themselves—may feel it is wiser to steer clear of any activity, including sex, that could jeopardize the pregnancy. However, I do not automatically preach the virtues of abstinence to my high-risk patients. I know that these couples are already under a great deal of stress that could be placing a strain on their relationships. Rather than saying no to everyone, in each case I weigh the psychological and emotional benefits to be gained by the couple in sharing the intimacy of sex, versus the risks to the pregnancy. In many cases, I believe that an educated mother-to-be, who knows how to read her body and care for her pregnancy, may be able to have sex without placing any undue risk on her pregnancy.

I have seen patients who, despite myriad difficulties, have been able to resume sexual activity once these problems have been corrected. Needless to say, I only recommend this freedom to women who are well aware of the early warning signs of trouble, and who I know will call me as soon as they suspect a problem.

Since I don't know all of you personally, I cannot assess your situations. Only you and your doctor can do that. All I can tell you is that you should be able to talk openly and honestly to your doctor about sex, and if he routinely tells all of his high-risk patients to abstain, you have a right to ask him to review your specific case.

Travel

As you probably know by now, I don't believe in placing any restrictions on the activities of expectant mothers unless there is a good reason to do so. Therefore, in most cases, when a patient asks me about travel during pregnancy, I usually say yes, provided that she follow certain guidelines.

First and foremost is timing. If a patient has a history of miscarriage, I advise her not to travel during the first trimester. If she runs into problems during this critical period, she will need prompt attention from an obstetrician who is familiar with her case. Therefore, I advise patients to defer any trips until the second trimester.

Depending on the distance that you are traveling, air travel may be more comfortable than a long automobile ride. Whatever your mode of transportation, be sure to get up and walk around every half hour or so to maintain good circulation and avoid leg cramps. And don't forget to eat well, drink plenty of fluids, and allow for frequent bathroom stops.

Once in the third trimester, I advise patients to postpone any major trips until they are beyond the risk of preterm labor, at around thirty-seven weeks. If you should run into problems during this period, you need to be close to a doctor who knows you and with whom you feel comfortable. If you must take a trip after thirty-seven weeks, be sure you and your doctor have planned for the possibility of delivery in an out-of-town hospital.

At no time in your pregnancy should you travel to a remote place that lacks appropriate medical facilities. I also advise patients to avoid places where they need to be concerned about the safety or cleanliness of the food or water supply.

Emotional Stress

Everyday stress or even a severe emotional blow is probably not going to dislodge a healthy, normal pregnancy. However, extreme stress can be devastating to a pregnancy that is more fragile.

Stress not only affects the mind, it can have an adverse effect on the body. An extremely stressful situation, such as a serious illness or death in the family, can interfere with the normal functioning of the endocrine system, which in turn could affect hormonal balances throughout the body. In the case of a precarious pregnancy, even the slightest negative change in the womb environment could lead to serious trouble.

This is not to say that every woman with a problem pregnancy is doomed to miscarry if she is under severe stress. All I am saying is that women with high-risk pregnancies should be aware that stress could be a problem. Fortunately, it is not an insurmountable one. It's important to remember that stress itself is not the culprit; rather, the problem stems from the way we react to stressful situations. Those of us who don't bottle up our emotions, and are able to reach out and talk about our problems with others, are better equipped to cope with stress than those of us who do. If you are experiencing a great deal of stress during a pregnancy, I advise you to find someone to talk to—your doctor, a friend, your spouse, or even a professional counselor. The worst thing you can do is to keep it to yourself. (For more information on coping with stress, read chapter 10, "With a Little Help from Your Friends."

Exercise During Pregnancy

In the past, for many women the worst part of pregnancy was being forced to refrain from any exercise for fear of harming their babies. Fortunately, today we know that for most women, moderate exercise during pregnancy is not only beneficial to their health and well-being, but poses no risk to the fetus as long as certain precautions are taken.

Call your doctor.   Before undergoing any exercise program, consult your obstetrician. Women who have placenta previa, abruptio placentae, hypertension, an incompetent cervix, a history of premature labor, ruptured membranes, a history of three miscarriages or more, or who are considered high risk for any other reason may be instructed by their doctors to avoid all exercise and must be extremely cautious about performing even the mildest exercise without checking with their obstetricians.

Don't strain your abdominal muscles.   Today, the woman who wants to remain fit during pregnancy can choose from any number of exercise books and videos. As a rule, these programs are geared for the perfectly healthy woman who is experiencing an absolutely normal pregnancy. The creators of these exercise regimes usually do not anticipate that some of the women who follow their programs may have hidden problems that will not surface until later in the pregnancy. Therefore, they include some exercises that can aggravate certain conditions.

I advise my patients to steer clear of any exercise that puts a strain on the abdominal muscles, such as sit-ups or curl-ups.

While these exercises may be fine for the majority of pregnant women, they can be dangerous for those who have an incompetent cervix, placenta previa, a weak placental attachment, or other problems of which they may not be aware.

Don't overexert yourself. Pregnant women should avoid doing calisthenics or any aerobic type of exercise that increases their heart rate beyond 140 beats per minute, or 23 beats every 10 seconds. If you push too hard, more blood may flow to your muscles, depriving the fetus of much-needed oxygen and nutrients.

Avoid becoming overheated. For the safety of your baby, you should maintain a body temperature of less than 101 degrees Fahrenheit. To keep cool, drink plenty of fluids, and stop exercising before you feel you need to. Stay out of hot tubs and saunas.

Stay off your back. Beyond the fourth month, don't do any exercises while flat on your back, because it will reduce the blood flow to the placenta.

Avoid any activity that increases your risk of falling. As your abdomen gets bigger, and your center of gravity shifts to the front, it becomes harder to maintain your balance. As a rule, it's best to avoid sports that require good balance, such as ice skating, downhill skiing, or even a heated game of tennis that sends you racing all over the court. If you're a very competent rider, slow bicycle riding is okay, but no racing.

Avoid excessive physical stress. Sports such as scuba diving, surfing, and water skiing are not only too stressful for the mother, but the consequences of an accident are too risky for the fetus.

The best exercises for pregnant women are the following:

1. *Swimming.* Swimming, which uses many different muscle groups, is a terrific way to stay in shape throughout

your pregnancy. An added bonus: Since your body weight is supported by the water, you're less likely to strain yourself.

2. *Walking.*   A daily walk in a comfortable pair of low-heeled shoes will help you feel more energetic and less awkward.

3. *Muscle toning and relaxation exercises.*   Gentle stretching and deep-breathing exercises will help keep your blood circulating, your muscles supple, and your body relaxed.

SEVEN

Emergency Procedures

I had two miscarriages and I spotted early in both those pregnancies. So when I started spotting again, I thought that all kinds of terrible things were going to happen. Every time you see any blood you think, "Oh, my God, I'm losing the baby." It doesn't matter how much blood, it could be a speck—that's all it takes to set your mind reeling. You start to panic even though you know that that's the worst thing you can do.

—Jennifer, carried pregnancy to term, giving birth to a six-pound daughter

*Y*ou're eight weeks pregnant and you wake up one morning feeling a bit under the weather. Your lower back aches and you're experiencing some slight cramping in your abdomen, much like you used to feel before you got your period. Since you're not really sick, you get dressed and go to work anyway.

Two days later, though, you notice some spotting and you think that you may be starting to bleed. Although the cramping and backache haven't gone away, they haven't gotten any worse either. What is the correct thing to do?

1. Ask a friend who has recently given birth whether she ever experienced similar symptoms. If she did and they passed, then you can breathe a sigh of relief and assume that everything will be okay.

2. Don't wait another minute. Go to the nearest hospital emergency room. You're probably going to miscarry and the earlier you get medical attention, the better.

3. Go about your business and hope for the best. The pregnancy guide that your friend lent you says that about 25 percent of all women experience some spotting or bleeding during pregnancy. Therefore, you decide to take a "wait and see approach."

4. Call your doctor immediately for further instructions.

5. None of the above.

Answer: 5. You should have called the doctor two days ago as soon as you felt the menstrual-type cramps and backache!

I never liked trick questions on exams when I was in school, so I must apologize for resorting to this tactic. I'm not trying to make anybody feel foolish, but I am trying to make a point, one that I feel is so important that I have repeated it throughout this book.

Big problems often start out small. The key to preventing miscarriage is to educate patients and doctors to spot these small problems before they become big ones.

Ironically, the doctor is often the last one to know when a patient runs into trouble. Before they will call their doctors, many patients will consult books (as I've stated earlier, many of these pregnancy books are filled with misinformation), check with friends, or try to ignore the problem in the hope that it will go away.

By procrastinating, however, you're not doing your doctor or yourself any favors. Although you may hesitate to call your doctor to report what seem to be minor symptoms, from your doctor's point of view the extra few minutes on the phone is time well spent if it can avert an emergency down the road.

A case in point is the woman from our quiz who wakes up one morning with menstrual-type cramps and a backache. If she had called her doctor that morning, he may have told her to rest for a day or two, drink plenty of fluids, and call him later in the day to report whether she felt any better. If there was a temporary instability in the pregnancy—for example, if she was dehydrated and as a result, her uterus was starting to contract—this simple treatment may have been enough to prevent the problem from snowballing into a major bleeding episode that could lead to miscarriage.

If, however, the patient's symptoms got worse, leading her doctor to suspect that she may have developed a more serious problem such as an inadequate supply of progesterone, he would have been able to administer the appropriate treatment before she was in the process of miscarrying.

The lesson to be learned is a simple one: Don't wait for an emergency to call your doctor. Notify him or her as soon as you feel that something is not right.

Early in your pregnancy, as part of your pregnancy plan, you and your doctor should discuss an emergency procedure to be followed as soon as potential problems crop up. Your plan should include a detailed list of symptoms to watch out for, as well as an emergency protocol to be followed on your own while you're waiting for your doctor to return your call.

Although each doctor may want to handle this differently, this is the procedure that my patients follow as soon as they suspect a problem:

1. *Call your doctor.* Let your doctor know what's happening. If your symptoms are severe, that is, you're bleeding

heavily, you're in pain, you're running a temperature, or you're experiencing other potentially serious problems, call any time of the day or night and make sure that the nurse or the answering service understands that this is a true emergency. Depending on your history and the severity of your problem, you may be instructed to go right to the doctor's office or to meet him at the hospital. If your symptoms are not immediately threatening, but are worrisome nonetheless—for example, you've noticed a thicker-than-usual vaginal discharge and a lower-back ache—describe the problem in as much detail as you can and leave a message for your doctor to call you back. Even if you've left a previous message, if your situation should worsen, call your doctor again with an update. Don't be afraid to be persistent. If the answering service can't locate your doctor (he may have forgotten his beeper), call the hospital and leave a message. I've had some enterprising patients who have even tracked me down at home, and given the seriousness of their problems, I was glad that they did.

2. *Stay calm.*   If you think that you're losing your baby, your first impulse may be to panic, but that is the worst thing you can do. As hard as it may be to control your emotions, try to stay calm. Your emotions can have a positive or a negative effect on your body. For instance, if you're bleeding and you're under a great deal of stress, your uterus may respond by contracting even more vigorously, which could lead to more bleeding. If you relax, however—put your feet up, drink some fluid, take a few deep breaths, turn on some soothing music, and try to stay calm—the bleeding may subside. Reaching out for emotional support at a time like this can also be beneficial. Pick up the phone and call a good friend or a relative who will have a positive, calming effect. Have your husband come home from work and hold your hand. But whatever you do, don't immediately assume that the situation is hopeless. Keep in mind that a lot of pregnancies run into trouble, and many of them turn out to be successful anyway.

3. *Rest.*   As soon as you suspect a problem, try to eliminate any physical stress. Even if your symptoms are very slight, and

you don't want to spend the day in bed, try to rest as much as possible and avoid overexerting yourself. This is not the day to go to an exercise class or to push your way into a crowded subway to get to work. If you're bleeding, your best bet is to spend the day in bed. When you're off your feet, you're not only putting less strain on your uterus and cervix, but you're also increasing the flow of oxygen and nutrients to the fetus. WARNING: IF YOU HAVE A TILTED UTERUS, YOU SHOULD LIE ON YOUR STOMACH, NOT ON YOUR BACK. Although your bleeding or pain may not be related to your uterus, there's always a chance that it is. In the event that your uterus is not falling correctly, lying on your stomach will help push it forward. Lying on your back will only exacerbate the situation.

4. *Drink extra fluids.* As I said earlier, dehydration may contribute to the onset of uterine cramps. No one knows for sure why this happens, although some doctors speculate that the cramping may be caused by a high concentration of the hormone oxytocin in the blood. By increasing fluid intake, you're in turn increasing your blood volume and diluting the adverse effects of the hormone. Acid-type liquids such as cranberry juice may be of added benefit if you have a urinary tract infection.

5. *Write it down.* In anticipation of your doctor's call, write down any symptoms you may be feeling. Be as specific as possible. Since he may not have his records in front of him, be prepared to tell him the exact duration of your pregnancy (dated from the first day of your last menstrual period) as well as anything else in your history that is relevant, such as hypertension, previous miscarriage, or previous bleeding episodes.

When your doctor calls you back, he will probably have a lot of questions. First, he will want to rule out the most serious problems, including the possibility of an ectopic or tubal pregnancy, or a ruptured ovarian cyst. If you complain of abdominal pain, be specific about the location of the pain (left side, right side, high, low, or toward the lower back), frequency of pain, and whether any particular movement or activity makes it worse. If your doctor suspects a life-threatening situation, such as a tubal pregnancy or a ruptured ovarian cyst, he will want to see you immediately.

Second, your doctor will want to know about any other symptoms, such as nausea, vomiting, unusual vaginal discharge, bleeding, diarrhea, dizziness, fainting, fever, shoulder pain (caused by pressure on the diaphragm that could signal an ectopic pregnancy), or anything else that can help him reach a diagnosis. At this point, he doesn't know if a maternal illness is complicating the pregnancy or if the pregnancy is developing complications on its own.

If you're bleeding, your doctor will want to know how much blood is being lost. To determine the amount of blood flow, he'll ask you how often you have to change your sanitary napkin. The rule of thumb is that if you have to change a standard napkin more than once every half hour, your bleeding is considered to be very heavy.

Depending on the severity of your symptoms, your doctor may ask you to come right to the office, or he may tell you to continue your emergency protocol at home (plenty of bed rest and fluids) and call back in three or four hours with a progress report. In some cases, your doctor may prescribe medication, such as aspirin, to help alleviate the cramping and the bleeding. If there's no improvement by your next phone call, he will probably want to examine you.

The Emergency Office Visit

The internal exam   The internal exam can help determine whether the cervix has dilated or opened, or whether the amniotic membranes have been ruptured. If the cervix is closed, and the membranes are intact, the pregnancy stands a good chance of survival. If the cervix has started to open, it could be a sign of an incompetent cervix or it could also indicate that uterine contractions are forcing the cervix open.

In the first trimester, if the cervix has started to dilate and the membranes have ruptured, there's virtually no chance of saving the pregnancy. This is called an inevitable abortion. If the cervix is substantially dilated, it is also extremely difficult to prevent a miscarriage. (If this happens later in the pregnancy, steps can be taken to delay labor. See the section on the treatment for premature ruptured membranes in chapter 9, "New Hope for Problem Pregnancies.")

The internal exam might also reveal an infection that may be threatening the pregnancy.

Serum beta HCG test The doctor will order a serum beta HCG, a simple blood test to measure the amount of pregnancy hormone, human chorionic gonadotropin, in the blood. From that measurement, he can determine if the pregnancy is progressing normally. If the reading is low, he may suspect fetal death, an ectopic pregnancy, or a nonviable pregnancy in which there is no growing fetus. A higher than normal reading could indicate a multiple birth or a molar pregnancy, a rare condition in which the placenta is overrun by cysts and an embryo never develops.

Ultrasound Your doctor may perform an ultrasound examination to (1) check the location of the pregnancy if he suspects it could be ectopic, and/or (2) check to see if the fetus is still alive and if the pregnancy appears to be progressing normally. At about four weeks after conception, an ultrasound of a normal pregnancy will show a perfectly round, ringlike structure. Later in the pregnancy, an ultrasound will reveal whether a fetus is developing normally based on appearance, size, movement, amount of amniotic fluid, and heartbeat.

If the ultrasound reveals fetal death or a serious malformation, in all likelihood no steps will be taken to avert a threatened abortion or an impending miscarriage. In this case, the mother and the doctor may decide to let nature take its course.

If, however, all the tests indicate that for some reason, a perfectly healthy fetus is at risk of being miscarried, the doctor may suggest possible courses of treatment. If he doesn't, and the mother is intent on saving the pregnancy, she should make her feelings known. If her doctor is uncooperative or doesn't appear to be particularly knowledgeable, the mother should seek a second opinion as quickly as possible, preferably from a specialist in high-risk pregnancies.

If You Start to Miscarry at Home

Minor symptoms may take a turn for the worse. Or, maybe without any warning, you start to cramp and bleed heavily. No matter what you do, the bleeding doesn't let up. You may be having a miscarriage, and depending on the stage of your pregnancy, you may be expelling blood clots or actual bits of fetal and placental tissue.

As difficult as this may be, collect whatever tissue or blood samples you can in a clean container and store them in a cool place until you see your doctor (which should be within the next few hours). As we discussed in chapter 3, these samples could provide valuable information that could help with your next pregnancy.

By now, I assume that you know you must call your doctor at the first sign of bleeding. In this case, he will want to see you to make sure that you're not developing any complications and that, if you are miscarrying, all the pregnancy material has been passed. In early miscarriages—that is, those occurring before the tenth week—the fetus and the placenta are usually expelled together.

An incomplete abortion occurs when part or all of the placenta is retained in the uterus after the fetus is expelled. (A missed abortion occurs when a fetus that has died is not expelled during the first half of pregnancy.)

If all the pregnancy material is not expelled on its own, a D and C may be required. If the uterus is not cleaned out, the mother runs the risk of developing a serious infection or hemorrhage.

How can you tell if the uterus is completely empty? A physical exam will reveal whether it's shrunken back to its small and firm nonpregnant state. If it feels soft or tender, or appears to be enlarged, there may be some pregnancy tissue left inside. A serum beta HCG test will confirm whether the amount of pregnancy hormone is diminishing, as it should, or whether it is still at a suspiciously high level, which would indicate the presence of pregnancy tissue. Before your doctor rushes to do a D and C, however, he should also perform an ultrasound to see exactly what is still inside. In the case of a multiple birth, which is not all that unusual in this age of fertility drugs, it is possible for the mother to have lost one fetus but still be carrying another.

EIGHT

Inside the Womb: Keeping Track of Your Baby from Conception to Birth

I've spent a great deal of time teaching you how to read your own body and how to monitor your pregnancy, so that you'll be able to alert your doctor at the first sign of trouble. In this chapter, I'll turn to what your doctor can do to monitor the progress of your pregnancy practically from conception to delivery, using the most up-to-date technology available.

First Half of Pregnancy

Serum Beta HCG Assay—Eight to Ten Days after Conception

I can hardly believe it—to find out twelve days after conception that I'm pregnant. It's incredible!

—Sharon, mother of a one-and-a-half-year-old girl

This simple blood serum test can detect the level of human chorionic gonadotropin (HCG), a hormone released into the bloodstream by the developing placenta shortly after conception. The beta HCG assay offers significant advantages over the traditional urine test. For one thing, it is more accurate than the urine test. For another, it can be performed up to a whole week earlier. Perhaps most important of all, unlike the urine test, which merely verifies the presence of HCG in urine, the beta HCG provides specific information on the amount of HCG in the bloodstream.

Why is this information important? Any unusual variations in the HCG level can indicate a problem with the pregnancy. From conception on, the level of HCG should steadily increase throughout the first trimester. Every two to three days, the HCG level should double. For example, during the first week after conception, the HCG level should be between 5 IU/ml and 50 IU/ml. During the second week, the HCG level might be anywhere between 50 IU/ml and 400 IU/ml. The third week it might range from 100 IU/ml to 4,000 IU/ml, and by the fourth week after conception a normal reading would be about 6,500 IU/ml.

Anything significantly below average levels could signal a possible ectopic pregnancy, which if allowed to progress could endanger the life of the mother. A sluggish reading could also indicate a blighted ovum—a pregnancy that is not developing properly or one that is off to a poor start.

If the beta HCG level is somewhat higher than normal, it could be the result of a multiple pregnancy, that is, more than one gestational sac, as in the case of twins or triplets. However, if it is extremely high, it could signify a hydatidiform (cystlike) mole or a molar pregnancy, a rare condition in which the placenta forms cysts and an embryo never develops. Such a pregnancy is not only defective, it is also potentially very dangerous. Occasionally, a mole may turn into a cancer. Fortunately, it is treatable and curable.

When the beta HCG was first developed, it was considerably more expensive than the traditional urine test and therefore it was used very selectively. Today, the cost of the test has dropped because many more physicians routinely use it to confirm a suspected pregnancy and because of advanced technology.

Because of the valuable information that can be gained from the beta HCG, I perform this test for all my patients at about four weeks after conception, or six weeks after the first day of the last menstrual period. Some patients, however, should be tested earlier. For instance, any patient who has had a previous ectopic pregnancy or who is at risk of having one—anyone with a history of pelvic inflammatory infection or tubal surgery—should be tested as soon as pregnancy is suspected, and carefully tracked by her physician. I will also use this test as needed for any patient who, based on her past history, may require early intervention to sustain a pregnancy, or who is experiencing signs of possible miscarriage or ectopic pregnancy, such as bleeding, spotting, or cramping, or who has a medical problem, such as diabetes, that requires careful monitoring.

Urine Test—Fifteen Days after Conception, Day after Missed Period

Performed at home with a commercial home pregnancy test, at the doctor's office, or in a laboratory, the urine test detects the presence of HCG hormone in the urine, thus confirming the diagnosis of pregnancy. Unlike the blood serum test, however, the urine test does not provide any other information, such as HCG levels, that can help determine the viability of the pregnancy. If performed correctly, it offers a high degree of accuracy, although it is still less reliable than the serum beta HCG.

At this early stage, the confirmation of a pregnancy through a urine test is sufficient for most patients.

Ultrasound—Four Weeks after Conception, Six Weeks after Gestation Begins

The ultrasound technicians are usually stone-faced. They're not supposed to give anything away. I had been in the hospital for several weeks—it had been touch and go since the very beginning of this pregnancy—and by that time, we all knew each other pretty well. When we finally saw fetal movement for the first time, everyone got very excited. The baby moved her hand and it looked like she was waving. Suddenly, this doctor who is usually very businesslike started to laugh. "Look, she's waving at me," he said. Everyone started to smile. We knew that the baby was alive and well.

—Jackie, mother of a six-year-old girl

Of all the technological advancements that have made it possible for us to track the growth and development of a new life, ultrasonography, in my opinion, tops the list.

Ultrasonography enables us to safely look inside the womb without performing any invasive procedures or using potentially dangerous X rays. Ultrasonography is a process in which high-frequency sound waves are used to produce a picture on a screen or monitor. The procedure can be done two ways: the more traditional approach, through the abdomen, or a recently developed technique called vaginal ultrasound.

In the case of abdominal ultrasound, the physician moves a wandlike instrument called a transducer over the woman's abdomen. The ultrasound waves form sonograms or reflections on the TV-like screen or monitor.

Early sonograms were rather crude images showing general shapes and movements. Today, ultrasonography has been refined to the point where the pictures or sonograms provide a more accurate representation of fetal growth and development.

Vaginal ultrasound—which I believe will one day replace abdominal ultrasound during early pregnancy—provides an even more accurate image at that stage. A tiny plunger, about one-half inch in diameter, is placed inside the vagina. Since the ultrasound waves have less distance to travel, and pass through fewer organs, the pictures or sonograms are much clearer. It is also more comfortable for the patient. During abdominal ultrasound the patient must have a full bladder, since the bladder serves as a marker from which other internal organs can be identified. Vaginal ultrasound can be performed on an empty bladder, which makes it more pleasant for the mother-to-be.

If a woman is suspected of having an ectopic pregnancy or a threatened miscarriage, ultrasonography can be a very useful tool in determining the viability of the pregnancy. In the case of an ectopic pregnancy, early diagnosis could save the mother's life.

At about four weeks after conception, a sonogram of a normal pregnancy would show a tiny, ringlike structure forming a perfectly shaped circle. If the circle is abnormally shaped, it could mean that it is a blighted ovum, and for some reason the embryo is not developing properly. If a woman is bleeding and showing other signs of miscarriage, an abnormal sonogram would confirm that we should simply let nature run its course and terminate the pregnancy. At this time, we can also determine if there is more than one gestational sac, or if the pregnancy is ectopic, either growing in a fallopian tube or somewhere outside of the uterus. An ectopic pregnancy must usually be surgically removed, although, in a few rare cases, nonsurgical treatment may be possible.

By seven weeks, a sonogram will show signs of an actual fetus (or fetuses) and a fetal heartbeat. From this information, we can determine whether or not the baby is alive, although we are unable to rule out most significant birth defects.

Although most doctors feel it is perfectly safe, ultrasonography is not without risk. Some studies indicate that animals or cells exposed to high-level ultrasound could possibly develop cancer or birth defects. These studies, however, are based on much greater amounts of ultrasound than are typically used today. In addition, long-term studies of patients in Europe exposed to prenatal ultrasound show no adverse affects for either the children or the mothers.

Since there are still questions as to the safety of ultrasonography, I don't recommend it for everybody. In each situation, I weigh the potential risk—albeit small—against the possible gain. In the early stages of pregnancy, I would use it without hesitation, however, for the following:

1. A patient at risk of an ectopic pregnancy.

2. A patient who was bleeding or showing signs of a possible miscarriage.

3. A high-risk patient, such as one with serious hypertension or a history of miscarriage, who requires very careful tracking and early intervention.

Although the likelihood of an existing ectopic pregnancy diminishes in the second half of pregnancy, there are other equally serious conditions, such as the possibility of placenta previa, abruptio placentae, or even an ovarian cyst, that would warrant the use of ultrasound. Ultrasound may also be used to screen for neural tube problems such as spina bifida or anencephaly. (See twelve-week ultrasound exam.)

Prior to delivery, ultrasound may be used to determine fetal position.

Doppler—Six Weeks after Conception

> I knew I was pregnant before I took the test because I was
> so nauseous. Every odor made me sick. I had to force
> myself to eat. I was also exhausted and very anxious. But
> when I heard my baby's heart beat for the first time, I
> realized that all the discomfort was a small price to pay for
> this little miracle.
>
> — Liz, four miscarriages, mother of a three-year-old boy

A Doppler, a hand-held ultrasound device, can detect a heartbeat at around six weeks after conception for some, but not all, babies. Since babies develop at different rates inside the womb, it may take longer to find a heartbeat for some babies than others. Also, if the mother is obese, the layers of fat may muffle the sound. The presence of fibroid tumors or a backward-tilted uterus may also delay detection of the fetal heartbeat.

If a woman doesn't have any of these problems, and the heartbeat is not heard by the eighth week, her doctor should review whether or not she is experiencing any signs of miscarriage, such as cramping, bleeding, or spotting. If not, he may decide to wait another week or two before investigating further. However, by the tenth week after conception, regardless of any physical obstacles, the heartbeat should be apparent with the help of a Doppler. If by then the heartbeat is still not evident, it would be appropriate to perform an ultrasound to see if the baby is still alive.

Chorionic Villi Sampling or Biopsy—Six to Eight Weeks after Conception

A chorionic biopsy is used to detect hundreds of chromosonal and biochemical abnormalities in the embryo or fetus. It can also reveal the sex of the child.

Guided by ultrasound, a doctor inserts a soft, thin tube through the cervix or the abdomen to the chorionic villi, the embryonic tissue that later forms the placenta. A tiny sample of the chorionic villi is taken for laboratory analysis. When the procedure was first developed, it was extremely risky, resulting in complications that led to miscarriage in between 15 and 30 percent of all cases. Now, more than five years later, it is far safer than it was, but nevertheless, about 3 out of 200 of all women who undergo chorionic biopsy will develop complications, such as infection, that will lead to miscarriage. (The rate for amniocentesis is 1 out of 200.)

Although it is slightly more dangerous, chorionic villi sampling offers some real advantages over amniocentesis. For one thing, it can be performed up to five weeks earlier. For another thing, chorionic biopsy provides quicker results than amniocentesis—as fast as twenty-four hours in some cases—eliminating what can be an agonizingly long wait.

However, there are some significant disadvantages. In addition to being somewhat riskier than amniocentesis, chorionic villi sampling does not detect neural tube defects such as spina bifida or anencephaly. Also, since it is still relatively new, chorionic biopsy is only performed at major medical centers throughout the United States and may not be available to many women. Even in areas where it is, doctors usually recommend it only for patients with problem histories, such as a couple with a previous Down's syndrome child or other suspected chromosomal or biochemical abnormality.

Ultrasound—Twelve Weeks

By the twelfth week, through ultrasonography, doctors can now see the outline of the entire baby from his head to his toes, which gives them a good idea of whether the baby is developing properly. By this time, in many cases, they can rule out such serious abnormalities as anencephaly and spina bifida.

Doctors can also check the overall womb environment. Is the baby the right size according to his stage of development? Is he moving properly? Does he appear to be adequately nourished?

The twelve-week ultrasound can be a turning point in some pregnancies. A case in point is a woman with an incompetent cervix who was starting to show signs of miscarriage. If time allowed, to ensure that he was not saving a fetus that had little chance of survival, a physician might wait for the results of this ultrasound before performing a cervical cerclage, a surgical procedure in which the cervix is sutured closed.

Alpha Fetal Protein Test—Sixteen Weeks

This blood test determines the level of alpha fetal protein (AFP), a protein produced by the fetus as it grows within the womb. The AFP level increases as the fetus ages. An unusually high amount of AFP in the blood could indicate a possible neural tube defect such as anencephaly or spina bifida. At times, an abnormal AFP may also indicate that a normal pregnancy may be developing complications. A high AFP, however, could also be the result of a multiple pregnancy, or it could mean the pregnancy has progressed further than was first believed.

If the first AFP test comes back abnormal, a second one is performed to rule out possible errors. If the second test is still high, the doctor will probably want to perform an ultrasound to check for any visible neural tube defects, fetal viability, or a possible multiple pregnancy. Sometimes the ultrasound may be inconclusive, in which case the couple may opt for an amniocentesis. A high level of AFP in the amniotic fluid may confirm a diagnosis of spina bifida.

Many women who test abnormally high for AFP will later find out that their babies are normal. Because of the high margin of error, AFP is somewhat controversial, although most doctors will perform AFP as a screening test to rule out certain problems.

Any woman who has had a neural tube problem in a previous pregnancy should definitely be tested because she has about a 1 in 20 chance of a recurrence.

Amniocentesis—Fifteen to Eighteen Weeks

> Because I was over thirty-five, Dr. Semchyshyn asked me if I wanted an amniocentesis. I said no. After three miscarriages, I didn't want to risk it. I had made up my mind that no matter what, I was going to have this baby. I didn't care if she wasn't perfect. I wasn't going to go through another pregnancy.
>
> —Jane, mother of a healthy, normal three-year-old boy

> The amniocentesis came back normal! After all I had been through—two stillbirths, one miscarriage—I finally felt as if I could relax and enjoy the pregnancy. My baby was fine.
>
> —Madeline, mother of two-year-old boy

Like the chorionic villi sampling or biopsy, amniocentesis is used to detect biochemical and chromosomal defects and can also reveal the sex of the child.

Through ultrasound guidance, a doctor inserts a long, hollow needle through the abdominal wall into the uterus. In what is usually a matter of seconds, a small amount of amniotic fluid is withdrawn. A local anesthetic is used and the procedure is usually, although not always, quite painless. Cells are then grown in a culture medium and analyzed for any defects. Results take up to three to four weeks, although some disorders, such as Tay-Sachs disease and neural tube defects, can be detected immediately through chemical testing of the amniotic fluid.

Starting from the later part of the second trimester and up until the end of pregnancy, amniocentesis may be performed to assess fetal lung development if there is a risk of premature birth, or to determine if there is any infection in the amniotic sac surrounding the fetus.

When amniocentesis was first performed in the 1950s, ultrasound was not available to guide the physician, and sometimes by accident the placenta or even the fetus would get punctured, resulting in miscarriage and other complications for the mother. Today, the procedure is much safer, although about 1 in 200 women will develop problems, such as infection, that will lead to pregnancy loss. In a worst-case scenario, a botched amniocentesis could even lead to a hysterectomy.

Although the procedure is usually safe, quick, and painless, there is always a potential danger of injury to the fetus and the mother, albeit a small one. Therefore, I would not prescribe an amniocentesis unless the mother was at risk of bearing an abnormal child and wanted to confirm the health of the baby prior to delivery. One must always consider risk/benefit prior to undertaking this procedure.

Amniocentesis may be performed on patients who:

1. because of advanced maternal age (thirty-five at the birth of the baby) are at greater risk of having a child with a chromosomal abnormality;

2. have a family history of birth defects or a previous child born with a chromosomal abnormality;

3. are at risk of bearing a child with a neural tube defect;

4. along with their spouses, are known or suspected carriers of a recessive gene disorder, such as Tay-Sachs, in which case their offspring have a 25 percent chance of inheriting the disorder; or

5. are carriers of an X-linked disorder, such as hemophilia, which the mothers have a 50 percent chance of passing on to a son but not a daughter.

In the case of sex-linked disorders, amniocentesis can identify the gender of the baby, but cannot tell whether or not a son has been affected. This information can be obtained through another procedure in which—with ultrasound guidance—a blood sample is taken directly from the fetus and the DNA is studied for abnormalities. Other hereditary diseases such as sickle-cell anemia and cystic fibrosis can also be detected through this highly sophisticated form of genetic testing.

Second Half of Pregnancy

Uterine Activity Monitor—Twenty Weeks Plus

An electronic monitor can also be used to document uterine activity if a woman has reported frequent contractions. As in the nonstress test, or NST, a belt or monitor is placed around the woman's abdomen and contractions are recorded on an EKG-type printout.

If a woman needs to be closely monitored for several hours a day, her doctor may prescribe a home monitoring device that she can operate by herself. A woman at risk of premature labor would wear the monitor several times a day for about a half hour each time. The monitor is linked by telephone lines to a central nursing station, where any contractions are quickly detected.

The benefits of home monitors are obvious: They are less stressful and more convenient for the patient because they allow her to remain in the comfort of her home or office.

Fetal Monitor or Nonstress Test—Twenty-four Weeks Plus

A fetal monitor is an electronic device that detects any variations in the fetal heart rate that could indicate illness or impaired health. This so-called nonstress test (NST) may be performed right in the doctor's office if the mother-to-be reports a dramatic decline in fetal activity or if she has any other symptoms, such as a sudden increase in blood pressure, which could threaten the health and well-being of her baby.

During an NST, a belt or monitor is placed around the woman's abdomen as she rests on the examination table or hospital bed. The monitor is linked to a machine that records fetal activity on a printout, much like an EKG. This safe and painless test records the response of fetal heart rate to fetal movements. In a healthy baby, heart rate should speed up after each burst of activity. If it doesn't, it could signal a problem, such as fetal illness due to infection or lack of nutrition. A sluggish heart rate, or one that can't maintain a normal baseline, is also a red flag that something is wrong.

If the results of this test are poor, the doctor has several options. If it is still too early in the pregnancy to even consider life outside the womb, steps must be taken to improve the womb environment. If the mother has a medical problem that may be interfering with fetal development, swift treatment could get things back on the right track. At this point, the mother-to-be may be instructed to get more bed rest or to watch her nutrition more carefully. In severe cases, steps might be taken to improve blood circulation to the placenta through drug therapy, or the doctor might try to give an intravenous infusion of sugar and water to the baby through the mother's blood supply. If the uterus has been contracting, he might prescribe a tocolytic agent (a drug that inhibits labor) to relax it, and thus improve the delivery of oxygen and nutrients to the fetus.

If it was late enough in the pregnancy—past twenty-eight weeks—a bad NST result would probably be followed up by a stress test, also known as the Oxytocin Challenge Test or OCT (see below). This test will delineate the fetal condition with greater precision. (In some cases, an ultrasound evaluation may provide more answers. See the section on biophysical profile, which follows.)

Biophysical Profile—Twenty-five Weeks Plus

A biophysical profile consists of an NST to monitor fetal heart rate, and ultrasonography. The ultrasound part of the

examination is a complicated procedure that must be performed by a doctor instead of a highly skilled technician. Since
it is both costly and time-consuming, a biophysical profile is
performed only on patients with suspected problems, on those
with a history of premature labor or stillbirth, and on those
with placental malfunction.

During the ultrasound examination, the doctor checks for
the following four items:

1. *Amount of amniotic fluid.*   An excessive amount of
amniotic fluid, a condition known as polyhydramnios, could
indicate that for some reason, the baby is having difficulty
swallowing, or is losing too much urine through the kidneys,
signaling a possible kidney malfunction. Excessive fluid is also
a sign of gestational diabetes, among other possible disorders.
Too little fluid, or oligohydramnios, could be a result of a malfunction of the placenta in which the baby is literally being
starved by lack of adequate nourishment.

2. *Physical activity.*   By observing the frequency and
type of movement, the doctor can assess the strength of the
baby. A baby that is in trouble will be noticeably weaker than
one that is healthy and robust.

3. *Position of baby.*   A strong, healthy baby will be in the
tightly packed fetal position and will occasionally kick or
move. A baby that is failing, due either to illness or lack of
nutrition, will not be able to maintain that tight fetal position,
and will appear to be limp or flailing.

4. *Breathing movements.*   Although a baby doesn't actually breathe while floating in amniotic fluid—he gets his oxygen through the placenta—he does make breathing-type
movements that change the shape of the chest or lungs. It's
almost as if he's exercising these organs in preparation for life
outside the womb. If the baby is weak or sick, he may not be
able to perform these movements.

A biophysical profile is performed late enough in the pregnancy so the baby has a chance of survival outside of the

womb—there's no point in getting a bad report if there's nothing you can do about it. However, even if a serious problem is detected, in certain circumstances measures might be taken to treat the baby in utero. For example, if an Rh positive baby being carried by an Rh negative mother was rapidly failing, a blood transfusion performed right in the womb could save his life. Or, if a maternal illness was believed to be harming the baby, the mother would be treated for the problem in the hope that the baby's condition would also improve.

The Stress Test or Oxytocin Challenge Test (OCT)—Twenty-eight Weeks Plus

The same device that is used to measure fetal heart rate in relation to fetal activity can also be used to measure fetal response to uterine activity. As the name of the test implies, the baby is subjected to stress by exposure to uterine contractions. If the mother is not having contractions of her own, labor-type contractions are induced through the administration of the drug oxytocin.

During an OCT, a mother is given three contractions in ten minutes. The test may take one or two hours to complete. The baby's heart rate is watched for signs of slowing down. If it fails to maintain a normal baseline, trouble is suspected.

While this test can be dangerous—once labor is started, it is not always possible to stop it—the information it yields is often invaluable. When the fetus is under stress, we can discover potential problems that would go undetected under normal circumstances. If we can diagnose a problem early enough, we might be able to correct it through treatment in the womb, or if that isn't possible, consider the option of early delivery.

An OCT must be done very selectively, since it can result in premature birth. At times, it can also be dangerous for the mother. For instance, if a patient with placenta previa goes into labor, she could hemorrhage. This test should not be used if the risk of hemorrhage or preterm delivery is too high. Under proper supervision, however, an OCT can provide valuable information that might possibly save the life of the fetus.

Nipple Stimulation Test—
Twenty-eight Weeks Plus

Like the OCT, this test measures fetal heart rate as it reacts to uterine contractions. However, unlike the OCT, contractions are induced naturally by the mother, who massages her nipples, triggering the release of oxytocin. There are both advantages and disadvantages to this test. On the positive side, unlike the OCT, this test is a lot less complicated because it does not involve the administration of any drugs. Since an IV is not required, there is no risk of bleeding or infection. However, on the down side, unlike the OCT, there is no way to control the amount of oxytocin or the resulting contractions.

Labor and Delivery

External Fetal Monitor

This noninvasive procedure involves the continuous electronic recording of the fetal heart rate during labor in response to uterine contractions. It is similar to the OCT, except this is the "real thing." The monitor is held in place by an abdominal belt. Although some hospitals have portable telemetry, in most cases the mother is confined to the hospital bed. A printout of the fetal heart rate will show signs of fetal distress.

Labor is inherently a stressful situation. With each contraction, the flow of oxygen to the fetus is temporarily interrupted. A normal, healthy baby should be able to withstand this stress. However, one that is starting to fail may not.

When the fetal monitor first came on the scene in the 1970s, many obstetricians embraced this device as a failsafe method of detecting fetal distress before the fetus was in serious danger. As I've discussed earlier in this book, the use of the electronic monitor coincided with a dramatic increase in the number of babies born by cesarean section. Critics began to wonder whether this technology was being overused, and whether the results were being misinterpreted by overzealous doctors who were intervening to "rescue" babies who really didn't need to be rescued. Some critics contend that the use of the monitor itself may lead to cesareans by preventing women from walking around and engaging in other activities that can help along the natural progression of labor. Still other critics of "high tech" childbirth feel that many hospitals may be cutting corners by using electronic devices to monitor women in labor, instead of paying nurses to do the job.

Although I am a strong proponent of technology, I also believe that technology should be used only when it is absolutely necessary for the health and safety of the mother and baby. There is no reason why a woman who has experienced a normal pregnancy should be continuously monitored throughout her labor. When one of my patients arrives at the hospital ready to give birth, I ask her whether she has noticed any change in fetal activity over the past few days. If she reports that her baby appears to be as vigorous as ever, I will put her on a monitor for an hour or less to make sure that her baby is responding normally to the stress of labor. If all seems well, I will then remove the monitor and allow her to do whatever she needs to do to get through the rigors of labor. Along with the labor nurse and labor support, I will carefully watch my patient, examining her periodically for any signs of undue maternal or fetal distress. If I feel it is necessary, I will ask her to wear the electronic monitor for short periods of time as her labor progresses.

I feel that my approach is a sensible one that takes advantage of technology, but does not rely on machines to perform tasks that are best done by people.

Internal Electronic Monitor

If the results from the external monitor are poor or inconclusive, we may need more accurate information before taking any action. In these cases, we may use an internal monitor, in which an electrode is attached directly to the fetus and the mother. In order to attach the electrode, the membranes must be ruptured and the cervix dilated at least one centimeter. As with any invasive procedure, there is some risk of infection to both mother and baby. Before this test is undertaken, the risk and the benefit must be carefully evaluated. In addition, before a cesarean delivery is undertaken on the basis of the results from an external monitor, this test should be performed in all but the most critical cases to confirm the earlier findings.

Fetal Scalp Stimulation Test

If the baby appears to be sluggish and the doctor wants to determine whether the baby is really sick or just sleeping, he will tickle the baby's head with his finger to see if the baby's heart rate increases. If the heart rate does increase, it is a good indication that the baby is well. This test is noninvasive and completely safe. However, if it is inconclusive or if the result is bad, a fetal blood sample may be taken.

Fetal Blood Sample from Scalp

If fetal distress is suspected, a fetal blood sample may be taken from the scalp to measure the pH or acidity of the fetal blood. A low measurement could indicate that the fetus is oxygen starved, and an expeditious delivery, often by cesarean, may be needed to prevent damage to the baby. Complications from the blood sampling include the possibility of fetal infection and bleeding. Although this procedure is not without risk, if a surgical delivery is being considered it is preferable to perform this test than to do an unnecessary cesarean.

In this chapter, I have shown how technology can be used to keep track of your baby's health and development. Unfortunately, this technology is often underutilized because many patients are unaware of its existence, and many doctors may not think of using it until it is too late to do any good. If you are concerned about the progress of your pregnancy, or suspect there might be a problem, don't be afraid to ask your doctor to make use of this extraordinary technology. Although a doctor will not order a procedure solely because a patient asks for it, in many cases a suggestion from an educated and aware patient may cause a doctor to reconsider his or her treatment plan.

NINE

New Hope for Problem Pregnancies

In the previous chapters, I have discussed how your body works during pregnancy and what can go wrong when it doesn't work correctly. In this chapter, I turn to the methods that we have developed over the years for dealing with problems in the event that they do arise.

Here I'll be talking about some of the diagnostic tools and remedies that are already well known, as well as some approaches that are on the cutting edge of science and technology.

Progesterone Therapy

Just a lack of hormones, it turned out, was why I was losing my children. All I really needed was two pills a day and plenty of rest.

—Sophia Loren, quoted in *Forever, Sophia,* describing the hormone treatment that she received after

two miscarriages; with the help of progesterone
supplementation and bed rest, she carried two
healthy sons to term

Progesterone is a hormone that plays a critical role in menstruation and pregnancy. After ovulation, the midpoint in the
menstrual cycle when the egg is released into the fallopian
tube by the ovary, progesterone is produced by the corpus
luteum, the follicle shed by the egg. This critical hormone
helps to build up the uterine lining or endometrium so it will
be able to nourish the fertilized egg after implantation. If the
egg isn't fertilized and pregnancy doesn't occur, the uterine
lining disintegrates and is shed during menstruation. If the egg
is fertilized by sperm, the corpus luteum continues to produce
progesterone until that role is assumed by the placenta.

After conception is complete and the ovum is securely attached to the uterus, progesterone serves as a stabilizing factor
that inhibits uterine contractions.

If a woman's progesterone level is inadequate in the second
half of her menstrual cycle, known as the corpus luteal phase,
the uterine lining may not be sufficient to support the pregnancy. Therefore, the fertilized egg or ovum may not be able
to embed in the uterine wall and will be expelled during menstruation. This is called a chemical pregnancy and the only
symptom a woman may experience is a late or unusually heavy
menstrual period.

If progesterone production is inadequate after the egg is
safely lodged in the uterus, the uterus may start to contract,
which could result in a spontaneous abortion. Since progesterone inhibits contractions, low progesterone production is a
factor in premature labor.

Progesterone insufficiency is difficult to diagnose because
the amount of progesterone needed to sustain a pregnancy
varies from woman to woman. For example, a blood test may
reveal that a woman's progesterone production is well within
the normal range. However, in her particular case, normal
may not be enough. She may need more progesterone than
her body is capable of producing. Therefore, I feel that in
diagnosing this condition, it is best not to rely solely on laboratory values, but to look further for other pertinent clues.

Progesterone insufficiency should be suspected if a patient has any of the following symptoms:

1. An early, unexplained miscarriage.
2. A history of menstrual irregularity.
3. While trying to conceive, has a history of late and unusually heavy periods.
4. Has a prior history of infertility.
5. During pregnancy, complains of menstrual-type cramps, spotting, or uterine contractions.

If I suspect that a patient is suffering from an inadequate supply of progesterone, I may prescribe a natural progesterone supplement, either in the form of vaginal suppositories to be used twice a day, or a weekly progesterone shot. In some cases, I will wait for the onset of symptoms (cramping, bleeding, etc.) before I prescribe the hormone. However, there are other times when I will begin progesterone as soon as a patient conceives, if her history warrants this kind of treatment.

The Risks versus the Benefits

WARNING. THE USE OF PROGESTATIONAL AGENTS IS NOT RECOMMENDED DURING THE FIRST FOUR MONTHS OF PREGNANCY.

— Packet insert, Hydroxyprogesterone Caproate Injection

You get a bottle of progesterone and inside there's a pamphlet telling you all the things that can happen to your baby if you take this hormone. I read it, and after that I said, "You want me to take this knowing what it can do?" And Dr. Sem said, "You need it. You will not go through a normal pregnancy without progesterone shots." I had already experienced three stillbirths. I finally said to myself, "It's worth the risk."

— Rosalie, carried a healthy baby girl to term in 1985

At one time, it was believed that the placenta served as a barrier, protecting the fetus from any harmful substances consumed by the mother. In the 1960s, that belief was shattered by a finding that startled the medical community. Many women who had taken a sedative called thalidomide early in pregnancy were giving birth to babies with seriously malformed limbs and other problems. Because of the thalidomide tragedy, we know that any drug that enters the mother's bloodstream can be passed on to the developing baby.

Drugs such as thalidomide that have been documented as causing birth defects are classified as teratogens. However, not all drugs have been shown to cause fetal damage, and some can be safely taken during pregnancy.

For over forty years, various forms of progesterone have been given to women in early pregnancy to avert threatened miscarriages. Some studies, based on research accumulated in the late 1950s, suggest that children born to mothers who took progesterone or progesteronelike drugs during pregnancy are more likely to develop malformations, including the partial masculinization of the external genitals in female babies or abnormalities in limb formation.

If you read the manufacturer's packet insert found with every bottle of progesterone, you will see all the possible complications that can be caused by taking hormones during pregnancy. Needless to say, some of them are very scary.

If progesterone is so bad, then why, you might ask, do thousands of doctors—including myself—still prescribe it for our pregnant patients?

The fact of the matter is, there are many different types of progesterone, and the kind that we use today is quite different from what was prescribed in the past. In the late 1950s, when researchers were gathering data on the correlation between progesterone and birth defects, doctors were prescribing synthetic or laboratory-produced hormones that were created from other components. While these chemically synthesized substances may have been able to fool the body into thinking they were the real thing, in reality these early progesterones were quite different structurally from the progesterone produced by the ovaries.

However, the progesterone we use today, hydroxyprogesterone caproate, is not a synthetic product. Rather, it is a purified version of a hormone extracted from natural substances. Since it is a natural product, it is similar in chemical structure to the progesterone that is produced in a woman's ovaries. The fact that this extracted hormone is so similar to homegrown progesterone may be the reason why more recent studies suggest that it is both safe and effective, especially when used to prevent miscarriage and premature labor. For example, one study done in Israel found that newborns of women who had taken natural progesterone in the first trimester as a treatment for bleeding did not have a greater rate of malformations than those born to mothers who had not received the hormone.

Another Israeli study documents the use of progesterone as an effective treatment for premature labor. In this study, women with a history of two miscarriages or two premature births were given weekly progesterone shots. A control group was given a placebo. The group that received the progesterone had a significantly lower rate of premature labor than the group that had not.

The decision to take any medication in pregnancy is a difficult one. No expectant mother wants to expose her child to any potential danger, especially one that could inflict a lifetime of pain and suffering. Whenever I prescribe progesterone, I urge my patients to read the studies carefully. Many are still deeply concerned about the impact progesterone will have on their babies. To assuage their fears, I often put them in touch with other mothers who, having used the hormone during pregnancy, can now boast of beautiful, healthy children, some of whom are in their teens. I remember one very nervous patient who not only wanted the names of success stories, but asked me for the numbers of women who, after taking progesterone, had given birth to malformed children. "I want to know both sides of the story," she explained.

It gave me great joy to be able to tell her that in my fifteen years of practice, I have never delivered a baby that was malformed due to progesterone intake during pregnancy.

Uterine Abnormalities

Retroverted, or Backward-Tilted, Uterus

About 30 percent of all woman have a backward-tilted, or retroverted, uterus. In most cases, these women will have no difficulty carrying to term. However, a small minority of these women will encounter serious problems. In these cases, as the pregnancy progresses and the uterus expands, the uterus tilts back toward the rectum instead of falling forward toward the abdomen, where there is room to grow. Eventually—usually around ten to twelve weeks after conception—the uterus becomes stuck and can no longer accommodate any more growth, resulting in a miscarriage.

Although it's easy enough for an obstetrician to spot a tilted uterus during an internal examination, it's difficult to detect which women will develop problems during pregnancy and which will not. Therefore, I feel it's advisable for any woman with a tilted uterus to be aware of the early warning signs that the womb may not be properly positioned.

Menstrual-type cramps, a mucous vaginal secretion (indicating that the cervix may be opening), and back pain during the first trimester are all signs that the uterus may not have enough room to accommodate the growing baby. If you experience any of these symptoms, alert your doctor as soon as possible.

Fortunately, if caught early enough, the problem can be treated easily. There are also some simple preventive measures you can take on your own. If you have a tilted uterus, when you become pregnant you should try to sleep on your stomach to help tilt the uterus forward. In addition, you should perform a simple exercise called a pelvic tilt. All it entails is getting on your hands and knees for about ten minutes several times a day. This safe and relaxing exercise, which can be performed up until the eighteenth week, will allow the uterus to gradually shift forward.

If, despite your best efforts, the uterus is still not shifting forward by itself, it may need some additional help. Sometimes a doctor will insert a rubber device, or pessary, into the vagina to push the uterus forward. The insertion of a pessary is a simple, painless procedure that can be performed right in the doctor's office. With the help of the pessary, eventually the uterus will expand to the point that it will fall forward by itself. At around sixteen to eighteen weeks' gestation, when the uterus is too big to fall back, the pessary can be removed.

If the tilted uterus goes unnoticed until it actually gets stuck, your doctor may have to push it forward manually and then insert the pessary. Although at this stage of the game this procedure can cause some discomfort, most patients agree that the momentary pain is preferable to losing the pregnancy.

Misshaped Uterus

The uterus is the organ that provides a safe environment for the new life from the time the fertilized ovum becomes embedded in the uterine wall until a full-grown baby is ready to be born. To perform this role, the uterus must be able to expand sufficiently to accommodate the growing new life. If the uterus is too small or improperly shaped, the fetus could have difficulty developing normally.

For instance, one of the most common of all uterine abnormalities is a heart-shaped uterus. In this case, the uterus may be divided down the middle by a wall or septum that could thwart fetal growth. This abnormality can be traced to a developmental defect in utero. Early in the embryonic state, the uterus develops from two halves that are later fused into one organ. For some reason, in some women, the uterus is not fully joined. In fact, in some rare cases, the uterus remains as two distinctly separate organs, accompanied by two cervices and two vaginas.

Some uterine abnormalities may have been caused by exposure to teratogenic agents early in fetal development. For example, women who were exposed to DES in utero, that is, whose mothers took the drug during their first or second trimester of pregnancy, are more likely to have developed problems in their reproductive tract, including a uterus that has an unusual T shape.

If a woman is born with a double uterus and a double

vagina, the condition can easily be detected during a pelvic examination. However, since the uterus cannot be seen without special equipment, most other uterine abnormalities are much tougher to diagnose.

A uterine abnormality, such as a heart-shaped uterus, may be discovered during an infertility workup if a doctor orders a hysterosalpingogram, or X ray of the pelvic organs. What makes it even trickier to diagnose is that there are no telltale symptoms, other than perhaps an unusual amount of uterine irritability during pregnancy, to help point to a diagnosis.

There are other more subtle clues that are sometimes overlooked. For example, in many cases women with abnormalities of the reproductive tract in general, and the uterus in particular, may also have a history of frequent urinary tract infections. Therefore, uterine abnormalities should be considered as a possible cause of miscarriage for any woman with a history of urinary tract infections who has experienced an unexplained pregnancy loss.

If a uterine abnormality is severe enough to hamper pregnancy, surgery may be required prior to pregnancy. For example, in the case of a double uterus, surgery can be performed to merge the two halves—each too small to support the new life—into one larger, whole organ. Or if a septum is dividing the uterus, the wall can be removed, giving the baby room to grow.

There are times when surgery may be too risky. Obviously, surgery is out of the question if the patient is already pregnant. In these cases, we must do everything in our power to ensure that the baby is able to grow properly by preventing the uterus from contracting and miscarrying the pregnancy. Fortunately, there are a number of medications we can use to relax the uterus and control contractions. Often, these drugs may tide a pregnancy over the difficult period, and uterine irritability may stop, allowing the baby to grow.

Asherman's Syndrome

This condition is characterized by adhesions, or scar tissue, inside the uterus caused by infection or excessive scraping of the uterine wall during a D and C. There are few symptoms, although Asherman's syndrome should be considered if a woman with a history of D and C has very light, scanty periods, has difficulty getting pregnant, or miscarries very early in pregnancy.

This condition may be detected through a hysterosalpingo-gram, through an ultrasound examination, or through a hyster-oscopy, a procedure in which a hysteroscope, a pencil-sized instrument with a light, is inserted through the cervix and enables the doctor to look inside the uterus.

A uterus that is afflicted by Asherman's syndrome resembles a house that is being overrun by cobwebs: The scar tissue has become so abundant there is no room left for the baby to grow. Surgery is usually required to remove the adhesions and can only be performed prior to pregnancy. Once the uterus is cleared of the excess scar tissue, the mother has an excellent chance of carrying her next pregnancy to term.

Fibroid Tumors

These benign tumors, commonly found in women over thirty-five, can be the cause of miscarriage or premature labor. During an internal exam, a doctor may be able to feel the fibroids as he palpates the uterus. They may also be discovered during an ultrasound examination, a hysterosalpingogram, or a hysteroscopy.

Outside of pregnancy, fibroids pose little risk. However, when a woman becomes pregnant, elevated hormone levels may trigger fibroid growth. If the fibroids become too big, they can interfere with fetal growth by robbing the baby of much-needed oxygen and nutrients, or crowding the baby out of the womb, thus causing a miscarriage.

Prior to pregnancy, fibroids can be successfully treated with medications that shrink tumors by inhibiting the production of hormones. There is one drawback with this treatment. It may temporarily interfere with the menstrual cycle, resulting in amenorrhea. Normal periods should resume, however, after the treatment is completed.

Fibroids can also be surgically removed through hysteroscopy or conventional abdominal major surgery.

Of course, neither surgery nor medications to shrink fibroids can be used during pregnancy. If a fibroid tumor is suspected of causing uterine irritability after conception, the only recourse is to prescribe medications to inhibit uterine activity, or lessen the pain if this should be the problem. It may also be necessary to improve the delivery of blood and nutrients to the baby by increasing the mother's nutritional intake and taking steps to improve circulation (see page 195 for more information on circulation).

Incompetent Cervix

An incompetent cervix is one that is too weak to support a pregnancy. As the uterus expands and the growing fetus presses down on the mouth of the womb, a weakened cervix will begin to efface, or shorten and dilate, as it would in preparation for labor. If the problem is not corrected in time, the cervix will give way and the baby will be miscarried or born prematurely.

Obviously, the trick is to discover the cervical weakness in time to do something about it. However, diagnosis is not always easy. Some women may have definite symptoms—a thick, mucous discharge, backache, cramping, spotting, or pressure in the pelvic area—but others may not have a clue that something is wrong. Therefore, any patient who experiences even the slightest symptoms should be monitored very closely.

Who is at the greatest risk of developing an incompetent cervix? Although it can happen to any woman regardless of her medical history, women who have had miscarriages, second-trimester abortions, premature labor, previous D and Cs, or who have been exposed to DES in utero, are more prone to this problem.

Prior to pregnancy, during a routine internal exam, a doctor may check for cervical weakness by trying to insert a small, pencil-shaped instrument called a probe or dilator through the cervix to the uterus. If the probe slides in easily, the cervix is probably too loose to maintain a pregnancy. An incompetent cervix may also be diagnosed through ultrasound or a hysterosalpingogram performed prior to pregnancy.

At times, a cervix that begins to efface and dilate during pregnancy may not have started out in a weakened state, but is responding to uterine contractions. At that stage, it's often difficult to pinpoint the exact cause of the problem. Nevertheless, it is critical to stop any uterine activity that could lead to premature labor, as well as to provide additional support for the cervix.

A weakened cervix may be strengthened surgically by a procedure called a cervical cerclage. If I know that a patient has an incompetent cervix, I will perform the procedure at about twelve weeks after the last menstrual period, or as soon as we can determine through ultrasound that the baby appears to be normal.

There are two types of cervical cerclage that may be performed: the more difficult Shirodkar method and the more common MacDonald suture.

The Shirodkar method involves inserting a quarter-inch-wide tape, made out of the same sturdy material used for artificial heart valves, deep into the cervix. It is a difficult procedure and requires a great deal of skill.

The MacDonald procedure is much simpler. The doctor uses a purse-string suture to close off the cervix and ties it shut with a knot, much like a small tobacco pouch that is closed by pulling the drawstring. Although this procedure is easier to perform, it is not as durable as the Shirodkar method.

Both procedures are performed under regional anesthesia—usually a spinal or an epidural—that numbs the body from the waist down.

My personal preference, and a method that I believe works better for most patients, is to do a combination of both procedures. Here's why. The cervix normally has two natural constrictions, an internal os and an external os. In the case of an incompetent cervix, both constrictions have lost their elasticity, much like a rubber band that has been overstretched and pulled out of shape. To properly correct the problem, both areas of the cervix need to be repaired. Although the dual procedure is more difficult to perform and requires greater skill, based on the positive experiences of my patients I feel it is well worth the effort.

One of the risks of performing this surgery late in pregnancy is that it may contribute to uterine irritability and trigger premature labor. Therefore, it is important to provide medication to inhibit any contractions during the procedure and until the baby is ready to be delivered.

The cerclage may be removed prior to labor to allow for vaginal delivery. If the baby is delivered by cesarean, the cerclage may be removed after birth. Although some doctors may keep the cerclage intact for the next pregnancy, I feel that in order to be effective, the surgery must be redone for each pregnancy.

Placental Problems

The placenta provides the fetus with vital nutrients and oxygen. If this remarkable organ ceases to function properly, the fetus could become malnourished and oxygen starved. Fortunately, if a placental problem is detected early enough, there's much we can do to improve the situation and maintain the health of the baby.

Placenta Previa

In a normal pregnancy, the fertilized ovum should implant on the upper portion of the uterus or womb, which is thicker, stronger, and more muscular than the lower half. However, in cases of placenta previa, the ovum implants on the weaker lower portion of the womb, causing the placenta to grow over all or part of the cervical canal or cervical os.

Complete or central placenta previa refers to a condition in which the cervical canal is completely covered. Partial or low-lying placenta previa means the cervical canal is only partially covered.

As the placenta grows and becomes heavier, the weaker portion of the uterus is not able to offer sufficient support. The placenta may stretch and thin out, and as a result, could tear and begin to bleed. Painless bleeding, in either the second or third trimester, is the only symptom of this potentially life-threatening situation for both mother and baby.

Any patient who is suspected of having placenta previa should be given an ultrasound examination to confirm the diagnosis. If the placenta has indeed implanted over the cervix, the ultrasound will reveal a bulge over the mouth of the womb. (A vaginal examination is usually not performed because of the risk of internal hemorrhaging.)

If the cervix is completely covered by the placenta, there is danger of serious internal hemorrhaging if the mother is allowed to go into labor. In this case, the baby must be delivered by cesarean section.

Until recently, a woman with placenta previa was told that her only recourse was prayer and bed rest. Unfortunately, even with that, the prognosis for a successful pregnancy was not good. Today, however, there are some extremely effective treatments that can help save these fragile pregnancies.

Although we can't do anything to change the location of the placenta, we can do a number of things to prevent uterine contractions, which usually cause maternal hemorrhaging and may lead to premature birth.

The type of treatment depends on the stage of the pregnancy and the exact location of the placenta. If placenta previa strikes late in pregnancy, with the placenta covering the entire cervical canal, the doctor must evaluate whether it's safer for the mother and the baby to try to sustain the pregnancy until term or deliver the baby by cesarean. If an amniocentesis reveals that the fetal lungs are mature enough for the baby to live outside the mother, and if the baby weighs the requisite 2,500 grams or 5.5 pounds, the doctor may opt for early delivery.

However, if a mother with placenta previa begins to bleed in her fifth or sixth month, before the baby can survive outside the womb, as is often the case, the doctor must decide whether he can prolong the pregnancy without too great a risk to the mother's life.

If the doctor feels he can safely sustain the pregnancy, the mother will be sent to bed until the bleeding stops. Bed rest alone, however, is not enough. Medication must also be given to inhibit any uterine activity that could lead to premature labor and possible hemorrhaging. Obviously, this expectant mother must also be taught to monitor herself very carefully for any uterine contractions and to alert her doctor as soon as she suspects that her uterus may be acting up.

With the help of medication, once the bleeding is controlled, the mother-to-be may be able to resume some of her normal activities until the birth of her child. In the case of a partial placenta previa, as the baby grows the placenta may move upward, away from the cervical canal.

Recently, some doctors, including myself, have reported excellent results after performing a cervical cerclage (normally used for an incompetent cervix) on women with placenta previa. A cervical cerclage is a surgical procedure, usually performed under local anesthesia, in which the cervix is sutured closed (see the section "Incompetent Cervix" earlier in this chapter).

Why do we perform this surgery for placenta previa? As the placenta grows and begins to weigh down on the cervix, the cervix may give way, allowing the placenta to expand. If the placenta stretches out too much, it could start to thin out and weaken. If the placenta becomes too weak, it could tear and start to bleed. However, if the cervix is given additional strength through the cerclage, it could provide better support for the placenta, preventing it from pressing down and thinning out and thus preventing hemorrhage.

Due to the delicate nature of the placenta, a cervical cerclage performed for placenta previa must be done very carefully because of the risk of bleeding and internal hemorrhaging.

Sometimes high risk can yield high reward. Consider the results of one recent study on the use of cervical cerclage for the temporary treatment of placenta previa. Twenty-five women, between twenty-four and thirty weeks' gestation, were admitted to a St. Louis hospital for bleeding due to placenta previa. Thirteen of these women underwent a cervical cerclage in addition to conventional treatment (medication, bed rest), while the remaining twelve received only conventional treatment. According to the study, the women who had undergone the surgical procedure were not only able to carry their pregnancies longer than those who had not, but had fewer complications throughout the remainder of their pregnancies and delivered babies closer to normal weight. (For more information on this procedure, you and your doctor can review a recent article by Fernando Arias, M.D., Ph.D., "Cervical Cerclage for the Temporary Treatment of Patients with Placenta Previa," *Obstetrics and Gynecology,* vol. 71, no. 4.) Also, in 1984, I wrote an article on the procedure, "A Double Cervical Cerclage: Treatment of Placenta Previa," *American College of Surgeons Surgical Forum,* vol. 35, p. 453. My personal experience with placenta previa and cervical cerclage in over fifty cases has been extremely rewarding.

Although placenta previa still poses a substantial risk for both mother and child, we've come a long way from the days of bed rest and prayer. With proper management, women with this condition have a good chance of delivering healthy babies without jeopardizing their own health and well-being.

Placental Abruption or Separation

A placental abruption occurs when the placenta begins to deteriorate and prematurely separate from the uterine wall. Depending on the stage of the pregnancy and the severity of the separation, the fetus could be deprived of oxygen and essential nutrients, leading to premature labor or even fetal death. As with placenta previa, the mother is also at risk of internal bleeding and hemorrhaging.

The symptoms of placental abruption include bleeding and abdominal pain which, interestingly enough, often occur in the middle of the night while the mother is sleeping. Because of this many women may fail to recognize or may totally miss these early warning signs.

Circulatory problems, such as low blood pressure, may also contribute to the weakening of the blood vessels that connect the placenta to the uterus. Since blood pressure may be lowered during sleep or when we lie on our backs, this may help explain why this condition often strikes at night.

If a doctor suspects that the placenta may have separated

from the uterus, he will probably perform an ultrasound examination to confirm the diagnosis. If the separation appears to be a minor one and the fetal heart rate is still strong, a combination of bed rest and medication to inhibit labor contractions may be enough to stop the bleeding. To improve the flow of nutrients to the fetus, the mother will be instructed to lie on her left side as often as possible. (It's okay for her to switch off to her right side if she needs to change positions, but she should stay off her back, as that will diminish the flow of blood to the fetus.) If the problem doesn't recur, the mother stands a good chance of a normal vaginal delivery.

However, if the placenta continues to separate chronically, the doctor will probably perform an amniocentesis to assess fetal lung development. If the baby stands a chance of being able to survive outside of the womb, the baby is delivered. At times, depending on the seriousness of the situation, an emergency cesarean is performed to save the mother's or the baby's life.

The consequences of placental abruption can be so devastating that the best approach is to prevent it from occurring in the first place. As I noted earlier, any problems of the circulatory system, such as blood pressure that is either too high or too low, may help weaken blood vessels in the placenta, which could result in a break or tear. Therefore, it is critical that blood pressure problems be detected early and treated as quickly as possible. (This is one of the reasons why I urge my patients to monitor their own blood pressure at home as part of my overall pregnancy program.)

If hypertension is diagnosed, medication such as Aldomet can be prescribed to lower it. If maternal blood pressure drops too much, simple steps can be taken to normalize it. For instance, the mother may be told to increase her intake of fluids, which would, in turn, increase her blood volume and improve circulation. In addition, nutritional supplements such as folic acid, vitamin B_6, and even fish oil tablets, rich in EPA (eicosapentaenoic acid) may be given to help bolster a sluggish circulatory system. Check with your doctor for dosages.

While placental abruption can happen to anyone, some women are at greater risk than others: specifically, women who smoke during pregnancy, or those who have had a previous D and C that may have weakened the uterine wall. These women, in particular, need to be vigilant about preventing the conditions that can lead to this problem, and detecting the early warning signs if it should strike. Needless to say, such pregnancies are at high risk and need close and skilled management.

Placental Malfunctioning or Insufficiency

An expectant mother may notice that her baby is not moving as much or as often as usual and her observations are confirmed by an NST. Or, perhaps during a prenatal exam, an observant doctor may notice that the fetus appears small for his gestational age.

A dramatic decline in fetal activity, or a fetus that is not growing properly, could indicate one of two things: Either the baby has developed a problem, or the placenta is not functioning properly, reducing the flow of oxygen and nutrients to the fetus.

An ultrasound examination of a baby will reveal if fetal development is progressing normally, or if the baby has a problem, such as a congenital heart or kidney defect, that could be making him sluggish or impairing his growth. If the baby appears normal, then the doctor may suspect that the problem is originating in the placenta.

A closer look at the placenta may provide some answers. An ultrasound may reveal a cyst or tumor on the placenta or an irregularity in its size or thickness that could be hampering its ability to function properly. For example, women with chronic and severe diabetes or hypertension have a tendency to develop placentas that are very small. As a result, they may not be able to provide adequate nourishment to the growing baby. In cases of gestational diabetes, Rh disease, or syphilis, the placenta is often swollen and enlarged due to water retention, which can delay the transport of oxygen and nutrients to the fetus.

An ultrasound may also reveal a rapidly aging placenta. Instead of developing normally over a nine-month period, for some mysterious reason the placenta begins to deteriorate before its job is done. If the placenta ceases to function, the baby could starve.

There are times, however, when, for no apparent reason, a perfectly normal-looking placenta will stop working properly. Whether or not we know the cause, as soon as placental malfunction is diagnosed, the doctor must quickly decide what, if anything, should be done. If it's late enough in the pregnancy that the baby stands a good chance of survival outside of the mother (at least twenty-eight weeks after the last menstrual cycle), the doctor will have to assess where the baby is better off: in the womb or in a skilled neonatal nursery. Additional tests, such as an NST, an OCT, and a biophysical profile (see pages 169–72) can help determine how bad things are inside the womb. If the situation is deemed serious enough, and the baby appears to be starving to death, he may have to be delivered by an emergency cesarean.

However, if the doctor decides that the baby is in no immediate danger, he may try to improve conditions within the womb environment in the hope of bringing the pregnancy as close to term as possible. If the baby is too young to be delivered safely, the doctor has no choice but to try to keep him alive inside of the mother until he has developed to the point that he can survive outside.

Here are some steps the doctor may take to improve placental functioning:

1. *Treat a suspected maternal condition.* If he suspects that a maternal condition, such as hypertension or diabetes, is responsible for the decline in the placenta, the first step is to try to control the problem. For example, in the case of diabetes, if strict control of sugar intake doesn't improve the condition, medication such as insulin may be required. If hypertension is identified as the culprit, once again, medication to regulate the high blood pressure may be prescribed. If a maternal infection is suspected of causing the problem, antibiotics may be used to clear it up.

2. *Eliminate external stress.* Bed rest—lying on the left side—can also help enhance the womb environment, especially if the mother is under a great deal of emotional or physical stress. Anything that can further aggravate the situation, such as smoking or drinking, should be stopped.

3. *Nutrition support.* Vitamin supplements, such as magnesium and fish oil tablets, may be used to promote better circulation throughout the body in general, and in the placenta in particular. Check with your doctor for dosages. Also, when it comes to food, this is one time a doctor may urge an expectant mother to throw away the scale and eat, eat, eat, as long as she adheres to a nutrient-rich, well-balanced diet. If the mother manages to gain an extra pound or two a week over her normal pregnancy gain, some of that nutrition may get passed on to to her baby.

4. *Glucose IV.* If the problem is very serious—the baby is too small to survive outside of the mother but is only hanging on by a thread in the womb—extraordinary measures may be necessary to avert fetal death. In some cases, the mother may be given a solution of water and glucose intravenously, that is, administered through a catheter inserted via a needle into the vein of the hand or arm. This serves two purposes: First, the baby needs the sugar to promote growth. Second, many women who have undergrown babies also have shrunken blood volume. The glucose IV will help expand the mother's blood volume and, in the process, improve overall circulation.

It usually takes a week or two before the baby shows any significant growth, although improvement may be noted in one or two days. During this time, while the mother is hospitalized, the doctor may also begin administering steroids (either hydrocortisone or methasone) to the mother to help promote fetal lung development in the event of an early delivery. In most cases, steroids are completely safe for the mother and baby. However, these drugs may increase the level of sugar in the mother's blood, which could aggravate a diabetic condition. In addition, steroids work as immune suppressors and could put a mother at greater risk of developing an infection.

While the glucose IV may be effective, it is not without risk. As with any other IV, the treatment may be painful for some women, and there is always a risk of infection.

5. *Medication to promote circulation.*   Blood is circulated throughout the body via millions of tiny blood vessels. If for any reason these blood vessels constrict, or if the blood vessels get plugged up—as in the case of hardening of the arteries due to cholesterol problems—the blood flow will be slowed down. If this happens when a woman is pregnant, the delivery of blood, oxygen, and vital nutrients to the fetus may be hampered.

To aid circulation, we may prescribe a medication that will help prevent the blood from clotting and in the process, improve the flow of blood throughout the mother's body. By doing this, we may be able to increase the blood flow from the placenta to the fetus. Medications such as heparin, a blood thinner often used to treat cardiovascular problems, and aspirin, which has a similar affect, may be prescribed. In addition, some labor-inhibiting medications, such as ritodrine and terbutaline (marketed respectively as Yutopar and Brethine), not only relax uterine muscles but offer the added benefit of dilating the blood vessels, thus improving internal circulation. Magnesium may also contribute to improved circulation.

Tocolytics: Drugs That Stop Labor

I had been a smoker and an occasional drinker. My
husband and I would spend the weekends partying. When
I got pregnant, though, I really cleaned up my act. I had
had two miscarriages and I didn't want a third. I ate well,
I exercised, I really tried to take good care of myself.
Everything was going well and then suddenly, one night, I
started cramping and bleeding. It looked like I was going
to lose the baby. The doctor gave me some medication to
stop labor. One of the drugs, Yutopar (ritodrine) made my
heart beat extremely fast. I felt very jittery, like I was
always on edge. Dr. Sem gave me some phenobarbital to
help slow it down. Then he gave me another drug called
Brethine, which wasn't even approved by the FDA for use
for premature labor, so I had to sign a consent form. I was
getting very scared that my baby was getting drugged. But
Dr. Sem told me that the worst thing that could happen

was that both of us might have a little withdrawal after
the delivery. Anyway, what could I do? I was six and a half
months pregnant. If I had delivered, the baby had no
chance of survival. So I kept taking the pills. At that point,
there was no turning back.

— Laurie, mother of three-year-old son, delivered at
thirty-six weeks

I'll never forget the night that a group of doctors—including myself, a young resident at a Canadian hospital—were
urging a woman in the early stages of preterm labor to drink
herself into a stupor. We cheered her on as she managed to
overcome her nausea and guzzle down a few jiggers of scotch
until she literally passed out. Back then, alcohol was the only
drug known to inhibit premature labor contractions. Alcohol
slows the production of oxytocin, one of the hormones produced by the maternal pituitary gland that causes contractions
and cramping of the uterus.

The treatment was unpleasant, to put it mildly. In order to
consume enough alcohol for it to be effective, the patient had
to drink enough to get her drunk. As could well be expected,
the mother suffered from a whopping hangover the next day
and complained of an upset stomach and a headache for several days afterward. What made matters worse was that after
all of that misery, there was no guarantee that the treatment
would even work. Fortunately, today we have a number of
medications to choose from that are more effective and less
stressful for the mother. The drugs that are used to stop labor
contractions are called tocolytics. As a rule, the success of these
drugs depends on the early diagnosis and treatment of preterm labor. The more advanced the labor, the more difficult it
is to control.

However, with early intervention, it may be possible not
only to stop preterm labor, but actually to reverse it. For instance, if the cervix has shortened or effaced too early in the
pregnancy, with prompt and appropriate treatment the cervix
may not only stop effacing, but may actually "grow" back or
return to a safer state. With proper treatment—medication,
bed rest, and perhaps even surgery to strengthen the cervix—a

woman who was going to deliver a severely premature infant at seven months may be able to carry to term or close to it.

Although there are a number of drugs used to arrest premature labor, only one, ritodrine (marketed as Yutopar), has been approved by the FDA for this purpose. Approved in 1980, Yutopar is a smooth-muscle relaxant that has a depressant effect on the uterine muscle, thus inhibiting uterine activity. This powerful drug belongs to a group of medications known as beta-adrenergic receptor stimulants or beta-mimetic drugs. Yutopar may be administered orally or intravenously.

Another drug in this group, terbutaline, marketed as Brethine (normally used to control asthma), has also been used to arrest preterm labor. Although terbutaline may be taken during pregnancy, the FDA has not approved its use as a labor inhibitor. Terbutaline may be used if the patient fails to respond to ritodrine or develops any complications due to the drug. It is usually given orally or subcutaneously (by injection).

Most patients who are hospitalized for preterm labor will receive their medication intravenously, through an IV. However, in some instances, depending on the situation, if a patient is educated enough to alert her doctor to a problem early on, she may be able to take the medication orally, avoiding hospitalization. This is not only more convenient for the patient, it spares her the added risk of infection and bleeding that can result from an IV. In addition, it is easier to control the amount of medication absorbed by a patient when it is administered orally than when it is given through an IV.

Recently, an innovative method of administering tocolytic medication has made it possible for women who would normally be hospitalized to manage their preterm labor contractions at home.

A tiny infusion-type pump filled with medication—similar to pumps used by diabetics—is inserted under the skin. A small, computerized device the size of a message beeper regulates the timing and amount of medication emitted by the pump. Thus, a patient can control when the medication is released, and the amount that is released, based on her individual needs. Needless to say, this system can only be used by an educated patient who is aware of her contractions either through self-monitoring or from information supplied by a portable electronic monitor.

The advantages to the infusion pump are obvious: The mother-to-be can adjust her treatment in response to her needs while remaining fully mobile and, most important, out of the hospital.

Patients who take either one of these medications may experience some alarming side effects, including heart palpitations, nervousness, perspiration, shakes, nausea, and in extreme cases, chest pains and pulmonary edema. The unpleasant side effects are often short-lived, and within two weeks the patient usually grows accustomed to these medications. At times, a tranquilizer such as phenobarbital may be prescribed along with these drugs to alleviate some of the troublesome side effects. However, if the dose is administered properly—that is, gradually increased over time so the patient can grow accustomed to the medication—and if the patient is carefully observed, the mother should not develop any serious problems. If the expectant mother simply cannot adjust to this medication, the doctor may try a different medication or a combination of drugs.

Most important, although expectant mothers may experience some discomfort, neither ritrodrine nor terbutaline appears to have any adverse effects on the fetus.

High doses of magnesium, a mineral that is naturally found in the body, may also be administered orally or intravenously to stop preterm labor.

Although magnesium also relaxes uterine muscles, it works differently from ritrodrine or the other beta-mimetic drugs. In the body, magnesium works as an antagonist of calcium. Calcium serves as a catalyst, facilitating the chemical reaction that is responsible for labor contractions. If the calcium is prevented from doing its job, then the process is interrupted and the uterus will stay quiet.

Taken orally in the form of magnesium gluconate or magnesium oxide, this drug rarely causes any serious side effects. If too much is consumed at one time, the patient at worst may vomit or suffer through a bout of diarrhea. Magnesium may also have a beneficial stool-softening affect, a welcome feature in pregnancy.

If taken intravenously in the form of magnesium sulfate, the drug is more quickly distributed in the bloodstream, resulting in side effects that range from minor to very serious. Women who receive magnesium through an IV may feel nauseated, warm, and flushed. Once the body adjusts to the drug, however, the discomfort should disappear. There is always the danger, however, that the drug may not only relax the uterus but also depress heart and respiratory muscles, which could seriously impair breathing and other body functions. Therefore, the patient must be carefully monitored for any signs of trouble.

Like magnesium, calcium channel-blockers interfere with the chemical reaction that triggers labor contractions by preventing calcium from entering the smooth-muscle cells of the uterus, and are a potent tool in the arsenal to fight preterm birth.

This group of drugs—which includes medications such as Procardia (nifedipine), often prescribed for heart patients—not only prevents uterine contractions but helps counteract some of the negative side effects, such as heart palpitations, caused by other tocolytics.

Prostaglandins are hormones that, among other functions, cause uterine cramping and contractions. Antiprostaglandins are drugs that inhibit the production of these hormones and therefore, indirectly, prevent the uterus from contracting.

Although these drugs have been widely used in Europe for several decades, and more recently, in the United States, to control preterm labor, they have not been approved for this use by the FDA.

The antiprostaglandins that are commonly used to stop preterm labor include indomethacin, a drug normally prescribed to treat arthritis, and plain old everyday aspirin, which many women have taken for years to relieve menstrual cramps.

As effective as these drugs may be, they can cause some undesirable side effects in both mother and baby. The mother may experience irritation of the stomach, which in extreme cases could lead to ulcer formation. In some women, these drugs may also decrease the bone marrow's production of blood cells, which could lead to serious complications.

There are also some potential risks for the fetus. Animal

studies suggest that exposure to antiprostaglandins in utero could induce major cardiovascular changes, including the premature closure of one particular blood vessel, the ductus arteriosus; such closure could cause fetal heart failure. Studies of women who took these medications during pregnancy to treat other problems, such as arthritis or kidney disease, show that they may be prone to longer labors and a higher rate of stillbirth than the general population.

Despite these potential risks, antiprostaglandins may still be the best choice of treatment for preterm labor if other medications prove to be ineffective, or when used in combination with other drugs. My experience has been free of undesirable side effects and recent studies have reported similar findings.

If these medications are used, both the mother and the baby must be carefully monitored. Various tests, including NST and ultrasound, will reveal the early onset of any cardiovascular difficulties or other problems that could lead to fetal illness or even death. The expectant mother should be given frequent blood tests to check for any change in blood count, as well as observed for bruises, excessive fatigue, paleness, or other signs of a reduction in blood cell production.

Premature Rupture of Membranes

I woke up at 3:00 A.M. because, suddenly, I felt very wet. My water had broken, but my baby wasn't due for another thirteen weeks. I was terrified. I called the doctor's office and left a message. He called me right back from the hospital. He told me to calm down and try to get some rest and to meet him in his office at seven the next morning. I couldn't sleep. I looked up prematurity in one of my pregnancy books. I read that at about twenty-seven weeks, the baby would probably survive, but there was a good chance that he would be blind or brain damaged. I started to cry.

— Helen, PROM at twenty-seven weeks, delivered healthy
  son at thirty-five weeks

Premature rupture of membranes (PROM) occurs when the amniotic membrane breaks before the onset of labor; it is responsible for 30 percent of all cases of premature birth in the United States.

Very often, the cause of the rupture is never discovered. However, maternal illnesses such as diabetes, infections such as herpes or chlamydia, retention of excessive amniotic fluid, and multiple fetuses are some of the factors that may contribute to PROM.

At one time, PROM meant that regardless of the stage of the pregnancy, or the baby's ability to survive outside of the mother, the baby had to be rescued from the womb. This sense of urgency was not unfounded. First, out of the protective amniotic sac, the baby was more vulnerable to infection, an extremely critical factor prior to the discovery of antibiotics. Second, without the amniotic fluid serving as a buffer, the baby could be crushed to death or deformed by any uterine contractions. Even if there was a chance that the baby was still producing enough amniotic fluid to protect it from contractions, prior to the discovery of ultrasound there was no way to determine if the baby's supply was adequate. Therefore, doctors had little choice but to deliver the baby, ready or not.

Many of the babies who were taken from the womb too early died during or shortly after birth. Many of those who survived suffered serious problems, including blindness, retardation, and brain damage.

Today, the story has a happier ending. Not only are we able to provide excellent care for preterm babies in advanced neonatal nurseries that enhance their chances for living healthy, normal lives, but more important, in many cases we are able to maintain these babies in the womb until their chances of survival outside of it are vastly improved.

Preventing delivery after PROM can be extremely difficult, but well worth the effort. Natalie, who called me frantically one night after her membranes ruptured at twenty-four weeks, is a case in point. Frankly, we were both worried. At that stage, the baby's prospects were grim: She had a mere 10 percent chance of surviving outside the womb, and even if she was kept alive, she stood a 90 percent chance of being blind and severely retarded.

Natalie and I felt that we had no choice but to try to sustain the pregnancy as long as we could. Fortunately, an ultrasound examination gave us some reason to rejoice. The baby, unfazed by the whole ordeal, was still producing enough amniotic fluid to provide a sufficient buffer. The sight of the baby merrily kicking away despite the potential threat to her life gave us both hope.

Together, Natalie and I devised our strategy. Since complete bed rest and close monitoring of both mother and baby were essential, Natalie was confined to a hospital bed for the duration of her pregnancy. During her hospital stay, we were constantly on guard against our two enemies: infection and contractions. To prevent the onset of infection, Natalie ate two containers of yogurt daily in addition to taking antibiotics as a precautionary measure. Since contractions could have put the baby in serious danger, Natalie was put on Yutopar and magnesium to keep her uterus quiet.

After a nerve-racking ten weeks, I decided to deliver the baby after an analysis of amniotic fluid revealed that the baby's lungs were mature enough to breathe on their own.

At 6 pounds, 3 ounces, Jennifer started life as a robust, healthy infant. A life had been saved, and a family had been spared the grief of a possible stillbirth or a lifetime of caring for a seriously ill child, not to mention the prohibitive cost of raising a child with a disability.

When it comes to PROM, prevention is still the best approach. If patients are better trained to alert their doctors to the early warning signs of the illnesses and infections that can lead to this problem, I feel we can significantly reduce the number of women who develop this complication.

There will be times when despite our best efforts, PROM will strike without any warning. However, even in these cases, I believe we can significantly reduce the number of babies delivered prematurely by providing prompt and proper treatment.

Bed Rest

I was in my seventh month and I started cramping. My doctor told me I had to stay in bed for a while until he was sure that I was out of danger. After two days of looking at nothing but the wallpaper in my bedroom, I was starting to go stir-crazy. I finally called my doctor and said, "Look, you may save the baby but if I have to stay in bed any longer, you're going to lose the mother."

— Jenny, mother of a three-year-old boy

At thirteen weeks, I was sent to bed because my cervix was weak and I started to develop some other serious problems. I had a career and I didn't think that I could stand being out of commission for any length of time. In fact, I was planning on returning to work as soon as possible after the baby was born. The funny thing is, I actually enjoyed being forced to relax. I spent my time reading about pregnancy, nutrition, labor, delivery, breast-feeding, and childcare. I became so interested in child development that I decided to postpone going back to work so I could care for our baby.

— Rachel, confined to bed for five months before giving
  birth to her son

Despite all the technological advances of the past decade, plain old-fashioned bed rest is still one of the most common treatments for preterm labor, placental insufficiency, premature rupture of membranes, and other complications of pregnancy.

Bed rest offers some real physiological as well as psychological benefits for both mother and baby. While you're at rest, the demands placed on your heart, kidneys, and other organs are greatly diminished. As a result, your body can concentrate more of its efforts on nourishing the growing new life.

Bed rest gets you off your feet, which in itself can help a troubled pregnancy. When you're standing in an upright position, gravity pulls the weight of the baby down on your cervix. As a result, a weak cervix may begin to give way, which could develop into preterm labor.

As for the psychological benefits, a regimen of required bed rest not only frees some women from the daily stress of working in an office or the rigors of running a household, but it also makes them feel that they are doing something positive to help sustain a difficult pregnancy.

However, for some women bed rest can be pure torture and may induce more stress than it's worth, particularly if staying in bed means losing a much-needed paycheck. Therefore, it's up to the doctor to weigh all these factors before sending a patient to bed for more than a few days.

We've all heard horror stories of women who have had to spend entire pregnancies in bed. Actress Sophia Loren is a case in point. In her biography, *Forever, Sophia,* she vividly recalls how after two previous miscarriages, she spent nine months confined to a hotel suite in Switzerland before giving birth to her first son.

Fortunately, thanks to excellent medications and other treatments, today it's the unusual patient who requires total bed rest. Even in my high-risk practice, only a handful of my patients have ever been told that they simply could not get out of bed for fear of losing the baby. In fact, if Sophia Loren had been my patient, I probably would have performed a cervical cerclage early enough in her pregnancy so that she could have been back on her feet making movies until it was time to deliver. (Unless, of course, she wanted to do that on the set!)

I have found that, for many of my patients, a modified form of bed rest—perhaps two to three hours a day—is enough to do the trick. For others, an afternoon nap will provide most of the advantages of bed rest without any of the emotional or physical problems resulting from too much time in bed.

However, there are times when it is much too risky for an expectant mother to leave her bed, even if it's just to visit the doctor. In these rare instances, I have accommodated these patients by making house calls. Although most doctors have long abandoned the practice of visiting patients at home, in some cases it is absolutely necessary for the health and well-being of the the mother-to-be and her baby.

Whether you're in bed for a couple of months or a couple of hours, to get the most benefit it's important to lie in the correct position. Most doctors recommend the so-called Trendelenburg position, with the bottom of the bed elevated so the legs are higher than the head. There are several reasons for this. First, if the legs are elevated, they're less likely to retain water and become swollen. The water that would have collected in the legs goes back into circulation, moving around the body until it is excreted in the urine. This not only improves the mother's circulation but also indirectly benefits the baby by increasing the flow of blood and nutrients to the placenta.

During pregnancy, it's best to avoid lying on your back because in that position the full weight of the baby is pressing on the same blood vessels that deliver blood and nutrients to the placenta. (Just imagine trying to breathe normally with a ten-pound watermelon on your stomach!) These vital blood vessels are located in front of the spinal column and behind the uterus. However, if you lie on either side, the blood is free to circulate through these vessels, which can better pump the blood back and forth.

Believe it or not, even a seemingly innocuous treatment like bed rest is not without risk. Patients confined to bed for extended periods of time may suffer bone and muscle deterioration, bedsores, blood clots, constipation, fatigue, and depression. In fact, according to a recent article published in the *American Journal of Nursing,* researchers estimate that the functional body loss after three weeks of total bed rest is roughly equal to the effects of thirty years of aging! Rest assured, unlike changes brought about by aging, the negative effects of bed rest can be overcome once you're up and around again.

Some of the adverse side effects of bed rest can be prevented by taking a few simple precautions.

1. To avoid exerting too much pressure on one part of your body, which could result in bedsores, shift positions at least every half hour.

2. To help promote circulation, take a few deep breaths every twenty minutes or so, and make it a point to wiggle your toes and fingers.

3. Ask your doctor about wearing elasticized or support hose, which can help prevent fluid from collecting in your legs.

4. To avoid constipation, increase the amount of fruits, vegetables, grains, and other sources of fiber in your diet and drink plenty of fluids.

5. Try to bolster your spirits by keeping your bedroom library well stocked and your telephone close at hand, and by encouraging friends and family to drop in at the time of day that you're most vulnerable to depression. (For many women, the hours from late afternoon to evening seem to pass the slowest.)

For a woman who is used to being active and involved in the outside world, the weeks or months spent in bed can be very difficult. However, she can take comfort in the knowledge that her efforts will go a long way toward increasing her baby's chances of achieving a lifetime of good health.

Immunological Disorders

Fetal Rejection

Women who have suffered repeat miscarriages for no apparent reason may have a rare abnormality of the immune system that causes them to reject their own babies, much the same way an organ transplant patient would reject a donated organ.

For some unknown reason, these women may produce white blood cells and antibodies that attack the fetal-placental unit, resulting in miscarriage. Although no one knows for sure why this happens, scientists offer several theories. Some believe that in a normal pregnancy, the placenta produces a substance known as blocking factor that prevents the mother's immune system from attacking her baby. In some pregnancies, however, the mother's body does not recognize the signals being sent by the placenta and calls upon its immunological army to attack what appears to be an unwelcome visitor.

Recently, one of my patients brought to my attention a newspaper article describing some innovative and promising treatments for this disorder. For example, at the Foundation for Blood Research in Portland, Maine, Neal Rote, Ph.D., of the University of Southern Maine, and Alan Donnenfeld, M.D., director of the Maine Genetics Service and the Prenatal Diagnostic Unit at Maine Medical Center, offer immunization therapy in which women are injected with white blood cells donated by their husbands. After receiving this shot, many of these women develop the blocking factor needed to sustain a pregnancy. Although there are no definitive answers to why this treatment works, Dr. Rote speculates that the women's systems are able to respond appropriately to the signals given by the fathers' cells, but not to those of their fetuses. A single shot provides the mother with the protective antibodies for up to a year or more.

Other groups throughout the United States are offering similar treatment involving injections of white blood cells from either third-party donors or from husbands. When this treatment was first devised in the early 1980s, groups that used third-party donors had a better success rate than those that relied solely on blood obtained from spouses. However, thanks to improved technology, a woman who prefers to use her husband's blood now stands as good a chance of success as those who choose a third-party donor. The overall success rate for this procedure ranges from 70 to 90 percent.

Immunization treatment is controversial and many doctors are quick to dismiss the immune factor theory as a cause of miscarriage. However, I feel that when a woman has suffered miscarriage after miscarriage and every other possible cause has been investigated and ruled out, the immune factor must be considered.

Antiphospholipid Antibody Syndrome

In some rare cases, women who have had multiple miscarriages may be suffering from a disease called the antiphospholipid antibody syndrome, a complicated name to describe a straightforward problem in which the victim's immune system turns against its own body cells. In pregnancy, antibodies may attack the placenta, depriving the fetus of oxygen and nutrients, resulting in miscarriage.

Women with this disease, which typically strikes during the childbearing years, may have a history of thrombosis or blood clots. Previous pregnancies may have run into complications such as hypertension and undergrown babies.

In less serious cases, one baby aspirin a day may be all it takes to sustain the pregnancy (see the section on antiprostaglandins on pages 199–200). However, in more severe cases where high amounts of the antiphospholipid antibody can be found in the bloodstream, a combination of baby aspirin, prednisone—a steroid—and heparin—a blood thinner—may be required to inhibit the immune response and maintain good circulation throughout the body.

In most cases, these drugs can be taken safely during pregnancy. However, there are some risks to both mother and baby. Since prednisone suppresses the body's immune system, women taking this drug are more vulnerable to infection and should carefully monitor their bodies for the first sign of trouble. Like any other steroid, prednisone could, in some cases, raise maternal blood sugar levels, resulting in diabetes. There is also some question as to whether prednisone may cause hypertension and low-birth-weight babies. In addition, animal studies have shown that taken during pregnancy, cortisone, another steroid, can result in a cleft palate. However, these animal studies have not been confirmed in humans. Nevertheless, a woman taking prednisone should work closely with her doctor.

Taken over a short period of time, heparin rarely causes problems in pregnancy. However, in rare cases, use of the drug could result in maternal bleeding and bruising. Since the drug does not cross the placenta, it does not affect the fetus.

TEN

With a Little Help from Your Friends

The Patient Network:
Women Helping Women

After what I had been through, I had no faith in doctors. I
thought they were all quacks. I didn't trust any of them.
When I found out that I was pregnant, I was a nervous
wreck. Talking to other patients made me a believer. I
realized that a lot of other women had had problem
pregnancies and now they had babies or they were so far
along, they could stop worrying. I didn't feel so alone
anymore. I thought if they could do it, I could do it.

— Mary, mother of a four-year-old daughter

About five years ago, I encountered a patient who
posed one of the greatest challenges of my career.
Ironically, compared with those of some other patients, her

case was not all that difficult. Mary had an incompetent cervix and an abnormally shaped uterus, two conditions that in many cases can be managed successfully. I strongly believed that with proper medical attention, Mary had an excellent chance of carrying a baby to term.

The problem, however, was that Mary did not share my optimism. In fact, she was convinced that motherhood was a dream she could never achieve.

A thorough review of her medical records shed some light on her pessimistic outlook. Mary had been pregnant three times before. In each case, she went into premature labor during her sixth month. All three babies died during or shortly after childbirth.

Devastated and bewildered by these three tragic losses, Mary finally sought the advice of other doctors. A fertility specialist suggested that her mother must have taken DES, which, therefore, was responsible for her problems. A careful review of her mother's medical history disproved this diagnosis. Another obstetrician correctly diagnosed an abnormally shaped uterus, but incorrectly told her that because of it, she would be unable to have children of her own and therefore should adopt. A third obstetrician advised Mary to have a hysterectomy rather than risk the emotionally wrenching experience of another stillbirth. Fortunately, upon hearing his advice, Mary walked out of his office.

For the next three years, Mary refused to see any more doctors. "I was terrified of all of them," she later told me. "I had been poked, probed, and hurt so much, physically and mentally, that I didn't want to let anyone else touch me."

One day, while shopping at a local supermarket, Mary stopped to admire a new baby being held by a neighbor. Her neighbor told her an astonishing story. After nine miscarriages, this woman was finally able to give birth. She attributed her success to the work of a high-risk obstetrician at a nearby hospital, who turned out to be me.

When I first met Mary, she was so traumatized by her past experiences that she didn't even want to let me examine her. So, for two hours we talked about high-risk pregnancy in general, and her case in particular. At the end of her visit, she agreed to come back the following week for an examination.

At our next meeting, after carefully reviewing her case, I told Mary that if she still wanted children, there was no reason why she and her husband shouldn't try again. In fact, with the proper pregnancy plan, I had a strong feeling that we would succeed.

Six months later, Mary called with the good news. A home pregnancy test had come out positive. Before I could even offer my congratulations, Mary confessed that she was absolutely terrified and started to sob. Concerned about her emotional state, and eager to start treatment, I insisted that she and her husband meet me in my office the next morning.

The following day I sat down with the couple and discussed the course of treatment. Based on Mary's history, I believed that she would require weekly shots of progesterone to prevent her uterus from contracting, as well as a cervical cerclage at about ten weeks to keep the weakened cervix from dilating. As I do with all of my patients, I stressed her role in learning about her body and monitoring it closely for any signs of trouble.

As I was describing in great detail how to check for contractions, I realized, much to my surprise, that Mary wasn't even listening. She was staring off into space, barely acknowledging that I was in the room. No matter what I said or suggested, she seemed determined to shut me out.

Suddenly, it dawned on me that Mary really didn't believe that she was ever going to have a baby and therefore was preparing herself for the agony of another loss. To her, I was just another doctor—or "quack," as she later confessed—who, although well-meaning, would end up hurting her just like the others. I knew that my partnership with Mary wasn't going to work unless I could somehow win her trust and, in the process, build her confidence.

If Mary didn't believe what I was telling her, I thought perhaps she would believe it if it came from a patient. I had just the right person in mind. Janice, now close to her ninth month, had sustained a very difficult pregnancy. Having suffered three previous miscarriages herself, she could well identify with Mary's fears and could perhaps offer some hope. I asked Janice if she would give Mary a call, and she was glad to oblige.

That evening, Janice and Mary spent several hours on the phone discussing their current pregnancies and their past losses. The results were astounding. The next day, when I called Mary to see how she was doing, I couldn't believe that I was talking to the same person. For the first time, Mary sounded optimistic and, more important, eager to take an active role in her pregnancy.

Mary wasn't the only one to benefit from the phone call. Later that day, I heard from Janice, who was very excited by the positive effect she had had on Mary, and offered to call Mary or any other patient who might need her help.

I took Janice up on her offer several times. Although Mary showed enormous improvement after our first meeting, she continued to be a very nervous patient who needed frequent reassurance. Whenever she seemed to need a lift, I asked Janice or other successful patients to give her a call. In fact, after she delivered a healthy baby girl, Mary confessed that she often tape-recorded those conversations so she could play them back in the wee hours of the night, when she would sometimes feel scared and depressed.

After I saw the positive impact of a few well-timed phone calls on Mary's life, with the help of my patients I organized an informal telephone network. Women in more advanced stages of pregnancy, and even some who have already delivered, now help others who may be experiencing problems.

The patient network can work wonders in helping women during critical periods. For instance, if a patient has suffered a previous miscarriage, during the next pregnancy she often lives in fear of miscarrying again at about the same time. During these emotionally trying periods, many patients respond very well to a supportive call from a woman who has also experienced these feelings, and who is now either enjoying motherhood or is on the brink of delivery.

Based on the positive experiences of my patients, I would like to see more obstetricians establish similar patient networks, not just for their high-risk patients but for any woman who needs extra support and reassurance.

Any pregnancy—even one that is perfectly normal—can be an emotionally charged experience for some women. Those who are trying to cope with the demands of a career, the needs of other children, or both at the same time, may be overwhelmed by the physical and emotional stress of pregnancy. A woman who has managed to handle these often conflicting responsibilities during pregnancy can offer advice and comfort to others as well as serve as a positive role model.

If your doctor doesn't routinely link pregnant patients up with other pregnant patients, you might ask him if you could help organize an informal patient network of your own. I think you will find that many patients would be eager to participate.

Coping with a Difficult Pregnancy

The hardest part for me was asking for help. I liked being an independent person who was very much in control. Suddenly, I found myself in need and it was very hard to admit it, and even harder to reach out to others.

— Laura, five months pregnant, mother of a
   two-and-a-half-year-old delivered two months premature

The restrictions imposed by my high-risk pregnancy created a major upheaval in my home. I felt very guilty. Not by the fact that the dust accumulating under the furniture was growing to the size of tennis balls or that most of our meals came from McDonald's. That really wasn't important. What really bothered me was the impact that this pregnancy was having on my four-year-old son. Were we selfish for doing it? Was I forcing my normally active little boy to curtail his activities too much because I couldn't keep up with him? Was it really worth what we were putting ourselves through?

— Audrey, mother of a one-year-old and a five-year-old

For many women, aside from a few minor inconveniences, pregnancy will have very little impact on their daily routine. It's true that they may be more conscientious about eating an adequate diet or getting enough rest—and if they're following my program, setting aside enough time each day to check for uterine contractions and fetal movement. In all likelihood, if they work outside of the home, they'll be able to continue on the job until close to their due date. If they're full-time wives and mothers, they may be able to run the household and chauffeur the kids around right up until the very first labor pains.

When a pregnancy runs into trouble, however, it's a whole different story. Suddenly, a woman who has been energetically pursuing a career or raising a family, or doing both, finds that her life has been profoundly changed by the prospect of losing her baby.

The lucky ones may be sent to bed for a few days and, if all seems well, may be allowed to resume some of their daily activities, usually on a lighter schedule. The less fortunate may be sent to bed for the duration of the pregnancy, and only allowed up for brief excursions to the bathroom or a quick trip to the doctor.

As a doctor, I am mindful that when I am forced to send a patient to bed—something that I don't do lightly—I am not only disrupting one life, but the lives of her spouse and children. When a wife, mother, and, these days, often a breadwinner is taken out of commission, it creates a void in a family that is not easily filled. The paycheck that was used to cover the car payments or the mortgage is gone. If the family can't afford to hire help, the jobs of chief meal planner, housekeeper, grocery shopper, and childcare specialist must be redistributed to others in the household or to willing friends and relatives.

Husbands, who often try to take on the additional responsibilities single-handedly, may feel overwhelmed and overburdened. Children may feel neglected. Expectant mothers who are confined to bed may vacillate between anger, guilt, frustration, and even embarrassment.

Even the best of marriages can buckle under the strain. In the words of one patient who, after several miscarriages, spent much of her last pregnancy off her feet, "We both may have desperately wanted this child. But neither of us anticipated how this pregnancy would pull us apart. In my exhaustion and determination to make this one work, I paid less attention to my husband and his problems and put my total focus on watching over the baby. Before the pregnancy, we used to share everything. Now, he's stopped telling me about his day-to-day problems and concerns. We both withdrew into our separate worlds."

I like to think that the joy I saw on both their faces when I handed them a healthy baby girl last year helped to reunite this couple after their long ordeal.

As tough as it can be, families in this situation can take comfort in knowing that there is an end in sight. Unlike chronic illness, pregnancy doesn't last forever and the ending is usually a happy one.

Through the years, I have observed that some patients survive through a difficult pregnancy better than others. They seem to be less depressed and their spouses and children seem to feel less put-upon. When I ask these women to describe how they made it through the rough times, invariably I have found that they share one trait: These women know how to ask for help, and if help isn't readily available, they will go out of their way to find it.

A case in point is Kim, a patient with a history of premature labor, who began feeling uterine contractions in the fifth month of her second pregnancy. In addition to prescribing medication to quiet her uterus, I advised Kim to get as much rest as possible until her due date. The only problem was that Kim was the mother of a two-year-old, who, like so many toddlers, was simply unable to sit still for more than ten minutes at a time. Money was tight, so hiring full-time help was out of the question. Kim didn't live near any close relatives whom she could turn to for help, nor did she expect her friends, all mothers of young children themselves, to be able to offer much assistance.

Determined to protect her pregnancy, Kim became extremely persistent and resourceful. Armed with a New Jersey phone book, she spent an entire day on the phone calling any charitable or nonprofit organization that could possibly offer any help. At the end of the day, after it had seemed as if she had exhausted all possibilities, she called her church. When she described her dilemma to a church volunteer, the volunteer came up with an innovative plan. Since it seemed too much to ask any one person to help Kim care for her daughter and her household, she would organize a group of volunteers from among the parishioners. Each one of them would commit an hour or two a week to either babysitting, cooking, or cleaning.

For the entire duration of her pregnancy, a cadre of about two dozen volunteers helped Kim maintain her family, and several stayed on to help after the birth of her son.

As it turned out, Kim was not the only one to benefit from her church volunteer network. Other patients in similar circumstances have followed her example by working with their churches or synagogues to recruit volunteers to care for themselves and, later, for other women undergoing difficult pregnancies.

There are some people for whom asking for help is a humiliating experience. It may hurt their pride to admit that they're having difficulty coping, or maybe they feel that it's an imposition to burden anyone else with their problems. While it's admirable not to want to shirk responsibility, it's foolhardy not to take advantage of whatever resources are available.

If used properly, friends and family can be a wonderful source of help. When caring relatives and neighbors call and ask what they can do, give them a specific assignment. With little extra effort, a friend can cook a meal as easily for two families as for one. A concerned grandmother can take a child to the park in the morning and bring her home in time for her nap, giving the expectant mother a good chunk of time to rest. A close friend or cousin can help clean the house once a week, or perk up a child who may be feeling a bit neglected by taking her on a special outing.

One word of caution: In your effort to plan enjoyable activities for your child, don't make him feel as if you're trying to keep him out of the way. Children are part of the family, too, and they should feel as if they're contributing to the overall effort. Children as young as three can be given their own set of chores, including such simple things as making beds or setting the dinner table. Remember, if your child is used to spending a lot of time with you, his life will be radically altered by your inability to keep up with him. If you can, try to compensate for his loss by spending more time with him reading, watching TV, or just talking. If you do this, when you do need time alone, your child will be much more accepting of another caregiver.

If you reach out to others, you will find that most people are more than eager to pitch in, especially for such a worthy cause. The best thing you can do for you and your family is to graciously accept whatever help you can get, and vow that when all of this is over, you will be the first to call and offer help to another expectant mother in need.

Reaching Out to Others: The Role of Support Groups

> At the hospital, they called it a "fetal demise." But to me, I had delivered a son, albeit stillborn. My husband was there with me. He held the baby. Then the nurse wrapped him up in some paper and took him away. I never saw him again. I went home about four days later with no support. When I said I was still upset, my doctor told me to take a sedative and the pain was supposed to just go away. Nobody understood how I felt.
>
> —Janet Tischler, founder of MIDS (Miscarriage, Infant Death, Stillbirth)

With few exceptions, most of the women in my practice have suffered a previous pregnancy loss of one kind or another. Some have miscarried after a few weeks or months, others have made it close to term only to experience the agony of stillbirth.

Regardless of why or when the pregnancy failed, nearly all of these women share one thing in common: They feel that the magnitude of their grief cannot be fully understood by those who have not experienced a similar loss.

For months—sometimes even years—after losing a baby, many women are still mourning the death. These women bristle at suggestions from well-meaning friends, relatives, and doctors who typically urge them to "stop dwelling on the past" and to "get on" with their lives. Even a successful pregnancy doesn't completely ease the pain. As one of my patients put it, "Nobody knew my unborn children. Only my husband and I ever actually saw them. As far as other people are concerned, they're erased from their memories. To them, they never even lived. To me, I lost three children. Even though I have a baby, I haven't stopped grieving for the three that never made it. I don't talk about it to many people because I know they cannot possibly comprehend what I'm feeling."

It saddens me to think that there are so many women in desperate need of support and understanding, who don't know where to turn. So, they withdraw into themselves, convinced that they must bear their burden alone. But there is a place to turn for help. All across the country, women who have lost children to miscarriage and stillbirth are finding solace from each other.

A case in point is Janet Tischler, a dynamic mother of three from New Jersey, who along with her husband, Steve, founded MIDS (Miscarriage, Infant Death, Stillbirth), a support group for families who have suffered miscarriages, sudden infant death syndrome, and stillbirths. I met Janet and Steve four years ago when I was asked to speak before their group. I found their story to be very inspiring because it confirms my belief—and one that I share with my patients when I ask them to join the patient network—that by reaching out and helping others, you can, in the process, often help yourself at the same time.

In December 1981, when Janet was twenty weeks pregnant, she made a routine visit to her obstetrician. The doctor was unable to detect a fetal heartbeat. An ultrasound confirmed her worst fears: For some unknown reason, the baby had died. A few days later, Janet went into labor and gave birth to a stillborn son.

Four days later, after Janet was released from the hospital, she was surprised by the reaction of many of her friends. "I was devastated. I couldn't believe how much I wanted that baby, but he wasn't here. He was going to be my fourth child and a lot of people said, 'Well, you have three already, what did you need another for?' or, 'He would have been born retarded, consider yourself lucky,' or, 'So what, you'll get over it.' They may have been saying these things to make me feel better, but it had the opposite effect. I was hurting very badly and I needed someplace to go with that pain."

Out of desperation, Janet called a clearinghouse in New Jersey that kept track of self-help organizations, to locate any groups in her area that dealt with pregnancy loss. A clerk put her in touch with Compassionate Friends, a support group for parents who have lost older children. Although Janet found the group to be very sympathetic, she didn't feel that it met the unique needs of parents who had suffered a miscarriage or lost infants shortly after birth. At the group's suggestion, Janet organized her own support group.

Through word of mouth, Janet located a half-dozen women in her area who had recently miscarried or who had infants who had died after birth. When the group got together, something wonderful happened. Women who had previously felt isolated and misunderstood finally had a place where they could find camaraderie and understanding. "We needed an outlet. We needed a safe place. We needed somewhere where we could talk about our feelings dealing with society. Dealing with being jealous of other pregnant women. Dealing with a spouse or a parent who didn't understand. Dealing with other children in the family," Janet explained.

After the group had met by themselves several times, they invited their spouses to join them one evening. For the first time, Janet's husband, Steve, spoke openly about the intensity of his grief, and how profoundly the experience had affected him. Much to Janet's surprise, he confessed that he had kept those feelings to himself because he believed that his wife and family needed him to be strong. "I did most of my crying by myself in the car, going from client to client. I still do today, but not to the same extent. But because I didn't outwardly show my feelings, Janet didn't think that I cared enough, or that I was being supportive enough. I was desperately trying to hold it in because I was afraid that if we both broke down at the same time, no one would be in control."

Janet and Steve weren't the only couple to discover they were having difficulty communicating openly after their loss. Other members of the group had similar observations about their spouses. "Through the group we learned that men and women may show grief differently, and the evening gave us a greater understanding of each other's feelings," Janet recalled.

As word got out into the community about the group, more and more women joined. While most of the meetings were informal discussions, on occasion Janet would invite experts, such as psychologists, social workers, or, in my case, a high-risk pregnancy specialist, to address the group.

Since pregnancy loss often affects the entire family—from children on up to grandparents—the group set aside special evenings for close family members and friends to discuss their feelings. "This was very important, especially for the siblings," Janet noted. "Many of them felt that they were somehow to blame for the death of their brother or sister, either because they may have played too rough with their mother one day or that they once may have wished that she wasn't having another baby. These kids feel very guilty and they need the reassurance of the group to tell them that they were not responsible."

Through the years, many members who have gone on to have successful pregnancies still attend MIDS meetings. As one member who is a patient of mine said with great annoyance, "Now that I have a little girl, I'm supposed to forget about the others who died. One child does not replace the other. My stillborn son was never buried; there's no grave to go back to. Attending these meetings is my way of memorializing his life and death."

Seeing women who have suffered previous losses become mothers can offer hope to those who are still trying to have children, or to those who are still too traumatized to even try again. "We have many women walk through our doors and they have said, 'I'm coming here, but I've just lost two children, or three children,' or, 'I've had two miscarriages or four miscarriages and I'm never having another baby.' I tell them, 'That's okay. Everybody grieves their own way. Everybody has their anger.' They sit through the MIDS program and in a couple of months, we have a lot of survivors in the group who have gone on to have children, and they see that others have done it and it gives them the courage to try again. That's the hope that a support system gives."

After a miscarriage or a stillbirth, there are both physical and emotional wounds that need to be healed. Sometimes, the body mends faster than the mind. It's important for women to know that other women like Janet Tischler are more than willing to offer help and support through these difficult times.

ELEVEN

Toward the Twenty-first Century

I have seen pregnant women of all ages and ethnic and social backgrounds profit from basic preterm labor education. The majority of women were able to recognize symptoms and then comply with recommended diagnostic protocols and preventive interventions. When caring, concerned health care professionals provide women with self-risk assessment tools at the onset of risk, newborn outcomes are favorable and the number of preterm, low-birth-weight babies is drastically reduced. The methods of prevention are simple and cost-effective to society, the family, and the newborn.

— Carol Peterson, R.N.C., M.S.N., perinatal generalist, St. Peter's Medical Center, New Brunswick, New Jersey

I devote a great deal of time in this book to teaching women how to take care of themselves during pregnancy, and how to differentiate between the normal "growing pains" of pregnancy and the more ominous signs of trouble. However, my purpose is not to provide a list of symptoms to be memorized or advice to be blindly followed. This book reflects a broader philosophy of patient care that I believe could revolutionize the practice of obstetrics.

This book is about redirecting the focus of obstetrical care from crisis intervention to prevention. It is about arming couples with the information they need to avert the loss of healthy, wanted children and to prevent the tragedy of premature birth. It is about encouraging patients to take responsibility for their medical care so that they can forge true partnerships with their health care providers. It is about teaching couples to become more informed, demanding and discerning medical consumers who will settle for nothing less than the best care.

In recent history, many of the major changes in the field of obstetrics have been brought about by consumer demand. For example, in the 1960s, spurred on by books such as Marjorie Karmel's *Thank You, Dr. Lamaze,* women began demanding the right to a drug-free, natural childbirth experience. Books such as the groundbreaking *Our Bodies, Our Selves* advocated the presence of husbands in labor and delivery rooms, and their full participation in the birthing process. In the 1980s, the skyrocketing rate of surgical deliveries in the United States spawned the Cesarean Prevention Movement, which has helped debunk the "once a cesarean, always a cesarean" myth. Initially, these grass-roots consumer movements were met with stiff resistance on the part of many obstetricians and hospital administrators. However, in a free society the marketplace prevailed, and health care providers realized that in order to remain competitive, they had to yield to consumer demand.

There is no doubt that the practice of obstetrics has changed for the better. Yet, much still needs to be done, especially in the area of preventing miscarriage and premature birth. Once again, I believe that change will come about only when consumers demand it. They must insist that their doctors begin to take prevention seriously. They must demand that their doctors provide them with the tools to carry their pregnancies safely to term and teach them the techniques to manage their pregnancies outside of the doctor's office. They must force their doctors to really listen to what they have to say, and to intervene on behalf of a pregnancy headed for trouble while there is still time to save it.

Preventing miscarriage or premature labor will not only spare couples the emotionally devastating experience of losing a baby or being faced with the prospect of caring for a child with lifelong disabilities, but it also makes sound economic sense. The woman who suffers a miscarriage frequently requires additional medical procedures and treatments that can run into the hundreds or even thousands of dollars. In addition, the loss of a baby can profoundly affect both the father and the mother, often interfering with their emotional well-being and even their productivity on the job. In short, everybody suffers. However, the cost of miscarriage is minimal compared to that of premature birth. As I have said earlier in this book, the cost of maintaining one premature baby in an intensive care nursery can run into the hundreds of thousands of dollars or even more. In fact, I know of some babies who ran up bills of over $1 million before even leaving the hospital.

Ignorance is certainly a leading cause of the high rate of premature birth. However, other factors can also play a role. For instance, half of all cases of premature birth happen to women from low socioeconomic groups who suffer from poor nutrition and inadequate prenatal care. About 9.5 million women in the United States are too poor to buy health insurance and are not covered by government health plans. By reaching out to these women, and by making proper prenatal care a right for all women—rich, poor, or middle class—we can drastically reduce the number of premature babies and prevent infant death and disability.

In the process, we can also save money. According to one recent study, we can provide adequate prenatal care for 149 women for the price of maintaining five babies in an intensive care unit! Another study shows that for every dollar we spend to provide good nutrition to pregnant women, we save three dollars by reducing the incidence of low birth weight, an important cause of prematurity. To me, that's a good investment because an investment in our children is an investment in our future.

Although our government may be dragging its feet in terms of ensuring adequate prenatal care to all Americans, corporate America is beginning to see the light. About 150 companies, including Pillsbury and Quaker Oats, sponsor a prenatal health program offered by the March of Dimes Birth Defects Foundation. The program includes information on recognizing the signs of preterm labor, the principles of good nutrition, and information on problems that can arise during pregnancy. According to *The Wall Street Journal,* one company reports that since it adopted the program, its employees' average medical costs for maternity and nursery care fell from $27,243 to $3,792 within a three-year period. In fact, according to the benefits administrator of the company, statistics show that for every week an expectant mother is kept pregnant, the company can save up to $10,000 in health insurance costs.

Given the fact that many women today spend more waking hours in the workplace than they do in their own homes, I would like to see more companies expand their benefits to include prenatal education. Women, who now constitute more than one-half of all workers in the labor force, should ask their employers or unions to consider implementing this kind of program. I believe that once employers see the cost-saving potential, more will be interested in joining the prematurity prevention movement.

My concern for the well-being of mothers and babies does not end on delivery day. I feel that it is critical that working mothers and fathers be given time off after birth to help their babies adjust to the world, and themselves to parenthood. I believe that parental leave is not a privilege but a right that must be extended to all parents, not just for the sake of their families but for the good of the country. On the most basic level, our nation is not a collection of states, cities, and towns, but a union of millions of families. If we are to enter the next century as a strong, secure, and competitive nation, it's time for our politicians to do more for the families of America than merely offer some nice-sounding slogans around election time.

As we approach the twenty-first century, we must recognize that the traditional family that reigned one hundred years ago is gone, probably forever. Most mothers work outside the home and for the sake of our children we must figure out ways to accommodate the needs of working parents. I look forward to the day when every baby, regardless of economic status, is able to spend at least the first three months of life being cared for by his mother or father. I look forward to the day when employers routinely offer working mothers—or fathers—flexible schedules, including part-time work, so they can strike a balance between career and family. I look forward to the day when addressing the needs of our nation's families becomes the nation's number-one priority.

My belief in the sanctity of life does not end when a baby leaves the womb. Every new life is a gift from God that should be cherished from pregnancy on through old age. Every new baby should be carried to term and given the best possible chance of achieving a lifetime of good health and happiness. Human lives are too precious to waste.

A P P E N D I X

Resources

The Bible says seek and ye shall find. I frequently quote this line to my patients because I believe that inquisitive and determined health care consumers can often find solutions to their problems, no matter how complicated these may be. The following is a list of self-help groups and health care organizations that may provide some of these answers.

For General Information on Pregnancy and Infertility

The American College of
  Obstetricians and
  Gynecologists (ACOG)
409 12th Street, S.W.
Washington, DC 20024-2188
(202) 638-5577

The National Foundation—
  March of Dimes
1275 Mamaroneck Avenue
White Plains, NY 10605
(914) 428-7100

Planned Parenthood
Western Region
333 Broadway, 3d floor
San Francisco, CA 94133
(415) 956-8856

Planned Parenthood
    Federation of America
810 Seventh Avenue
New York, NY 10019
(212) 541-7800

Serono Symposia, U.S.A.
100 Longwater Circle
Norwell, MA 02061
(800) 283-8088 (Infertility)
(617) 982-9000

Ferre Institute, Inc.
401 Columbia Street
Utica, NY 13502
(315) 724-4348 (Infertility)

Resolve, Inc.
P.O. Box 474
Belmont, MA 02178
(617) 643-2424 (Infertility and
    pregnancy loss)

Information on DES Exposure

DES Action
Long Island Jewish Medical
    Center
New Hyde Park, NY 11040
(516) 775-3450

Cesarean Prevention

The Cesarean Prevention
    Movement (CPM)
P.O. Box 152
University Station
Syracuse, NY 13210
(315) 424-1942

C/SEC Inc.
22 Forest Road
Framingham, MA 01701
(508) 877-8266

Herpes

The Herpes Resource Center
American Health Association
P.O. Box 100
Palo Alto, CA 94306
(415) 328-7710
Ask for the "Herpes and
    Pregnancy" fact sheet

Pregnancy Loss, Death of a Child

This is just a partial list of support groups for couples who have suffered pregnancy loss, stillbirth, or infant death. For more information on what's available in your city or town, call your local self-help clearinghouse or hospital for a list of relevant groups. If there are no groups nearby, you may want to start one of your own. Call your church, synagogue, or community center for help.

SHARE
St. Elizabeth's Hospital
211 South Third Street
Belleville, IL 62222
(Main office, has chapters
    throughout United States)
(618) 234-2120

Neonatal Bereavement and
    Support Group
St. Vincent's Hospital and
    Medical Center of New York
130 West 12th Street
New York, NY 10011
(212) 790-7508/7267

Aiding a Mother Experiencing
    Neonatal Death (AMEND)
4324 Berrywick Terrace
St. Louis, MO 63128
(314) 487-7582

Resolve Through Sharing
La Crosse Lutheran Hospital
1910 South Avenue
La Crosse, WI 54601
(608) 785-0530, ext. 3696

Helping Other Parents in
    Normal Grieving (HOPING)
Sparrow Hospital
P.O. Box 30480
1215 East Michigan Street
Lansing, MI 48909
(517) 483-3873

MIDS, Inc. (Miscarriage, Infant
    Death, Stillbirth)
c/o Janet Tischler
16 Crescent Drive
Parsippany, NJ 07054

Pregnancy and Work

9 to 5, National Association of
  Working Women
614 Superior Avenue, N.W.
Cleveland, OH 44113
(216) 566-9308

Occupational Safety and Health
  Administration
200 Constitution Avenue, N.W.
Washington, DC 20210
(202) 523-8148

VDT Hotline of the Office of
  Technology Education
  Project
241 St. Botolph Street
Boston, MA 02115
(617) 536-TECH

Index

Heredity, *see* Genetics
Herpes Resource Center, 229
Herpes virus 2, 30–31, 201, 229
Hiccups, 118
High blood pressure, 18, 19, 31–32,
     44, 60, 107, 116–17, 121,
     163, 191, 192, 193, 207, 208
  calcium and, 133
  exercise and, 146
  obesity and, 20, 129
  pregnancy-induced, *see*
     Preeclampsia
  warning signs of, 98
High-risk pregnancy, 14–15
  defined, 6
  see also specific problems
HIV virus, 29
Home births, 72
Home-care program:
  in first half of pregnancy, 121–22
  at start of second half of
     pregnancy, 122–24
  taking care of yourself, 126–48
     emotional stress, 145–46
     exercise, 113, 115, 127, 146–48
     nutrition, 127–38
     sexual relations, 143–44
     travel, 144–45
     in the workplace, 139–43
  after twenty-eight weeks, 125–26
Hormonal problems, 4, 21, 22, 24
  see also Progesterone
Hospital:
  delivery in, 70–72
  shopping for, 72–74
Huntington's chorea, 46
Hydrocortisone, 194
Hydroxyprogesterone caproate,
     180
Hypertension, *see* High blood
     pressure
Hypoglycemia, 128
Hysterectomy, 167
Hysterosalpingogram, 40, 59, 63,
     184, 186
Hysteroscopy, 40, 64, 184, 185

Immunological disorders, 42–44,
     206–8
Incomplete abortion, 7, 156
Inderol, 31
Indigestion, 95–96, 114, 126, 138

Indomethacin, 199
Induced abortion, 4, 36, 40, 41
  previous, 60, 185
Inevitable abortion, 7, 154–55
Infection, 4, 17, 26–31, 33, 40,
     63–64, 117
  incomplete abortion and, 7, 156
  from IV needle, 9, 194, 197
  missed abortion and, 7, 156
  patient history of, 60
  protection against, 137, 202
  susceptibility to, 132, 201, 208
  tests and risk of, 167, 174
  *see also specific organs and types
     of infection*
Infertility, 27
  history of, 21–23, 60, 178
  information sources, 227–28
  see also Fertility
Insomnia, 97
Insulin, 32, 33, 193
Insurance, 78–80
Intensive care nursery, 9, 79, 116,
     118–19, 193, 201
Internal electronic monitor,
     173–74
Internal examination, 154–55
Interview, post-miscarriage, 57–59
  checklist, 60–61
Intrauterine growth retardation
     (IUGR), 107
Intuition that something is wrong,
     110–11
Iron, 128, 129, 132–33, 138
Israel, 180
IUD, ectopic pregnancies and, 34

Jews, 46–47
Junk food, 127–28, 129, 131

Kidney problems, 25, 192
  impaired function of, 31, 32, 33,
     107
  infection, 99, 100, 101, 109, 110,
     117
Karmel, Marjorie, 223
Karotype, 49, 61
Kegerize, Joan, 50

Labor, 33, 70, 134
  drugs that stop, 169, 195–200
  dystocia, 18